PRAISE FOR WE'VE GOT NEXT

"These sermons from one of our nation's premiere preachers offer three great benefits to the reader. First, there is the helpful and long overdue focus on some of the women in the Bible whose lives were blessed by and were a blessing to Jesus. Second, there are the clear and often stunning insights drawn from the biblical texts that are proof that Gina Stewart is a skilled biblical expositor. Third, there are the lessons and applications that tie the struggles of those women in the ancient world to the issues and challenges faced by would-be disciples in our 21st century world. This is more than a collection of sermons, this book is a blessing to the church."

MARVIN A. MCMICKLE, PH.D.
President, Professor of Church Leadership, Director of the Program of Black Church Studies, Colgate Rochester Crozer Divinity School, Rochester, NY

* * *

"The sermons complied in this book have simmered in the mind and spirit of Dr. Stewart, and now, for the benefit of our consumption, been ladled out for our enjoyment. This book is filled with powerful messages that will speak to both men and women."

CYNTHIA L. HALE
Senior Pastor, Ray of Hope Christian Church, Decatur, GA

* * *

"This Book is a collection of Timeless Sermons that will enhance any preaching library. A must read for both men and women of faith. This book gives us the heart and soul of Dr. Stewart's passion for the preaching ministry."

CHARLES E. BOOTH
Senior Pastor, Mt. Olivet Baptist Church, Columbus, OH

"Undoubtedly, the Reverend Gina Marcia Stewart is one of the most pertinent, profound, and prophetic voices in the 21st century church, and this book of sermons is one that I am sure will inspire and positively impact all who read it. A combination of insightful social commentary, creative and sound exegesis, and clear Christian commitment, she has gifted us with a classic and challenging work that not only demonstrates an exciting womanist hermeneutic, but assuredly fosters spiritual growth."

MARGARET ELAINE M. FLAKE
Co-Pastor, The Greater Allen A.M.E. Cathedral, Jamaica, NY

* * *

"For most of the history of the African American church, the church subordinated women in clergy ministry and preaching roles. The tour de force of the preaching of Gina Marcia Stewart shows what the church has been missing all along. Thank God for this book as a record of one of the most gifted preachers ever."

FRANK A. THOMAS
Professor of Homiletics, Christian Theological Seminary

* * *

"For those of us, thousands of women and men in the many churches in this nation and throughout the world who have been delightfully, divinely privileged to witness the preaching prowess of the spiritually gifted Pastor Gina M. Stewart already know what it is to experience the good news of the Gospel in context through her fresh, insightful and relevant proclamation. Now in this tremendous volume of sermons, "We've Got Next: HERstory in HIStory!" we have opportunity to read and reflect again and again upon sermons designed and delivered to move us beyond the pew to practice in the marketplace."

CAROLYN ANN KNIGHT
Preacher, Professor, Social Justice Advocate, Smyrna, Georgia

To: My Favorite
Alpha Kappa Alpha Girl
Eunice
God's Not Done Yet!
Dr. V. Whitherd
9/24/18

WE'VE GOT NEXT

WE'VE GOT
NEXT

HERstory in HIStory

10 POWERFUL MESSAGES OF HOPE & TRANSFORMATION FOR WOMEN

GINA M. STEWART

FOREWORD BY RENITA J. WEEMS

MMGI
BOOKS

Published by MMGI Books, Chicago, IL 60636
www.mmgibooks.com
We've Got Next: Herstory in History
Copyright © 2015 by Gina M. Stewart

Except for quotations from Scripture, the quoted ideas expressed in the book are not, in all cases, exact quotations, as some have been edited for clarity and brevity. In all cases, the author has attempted to maintain the speaker's original intent. In some cases, quoted material for this book was obtained from secondary sources, primarily print media. While every effort was made to ensure the accuracy of these sources, the accuracy cannot be guaranteed.

Library of Congress Cataloging-in-Publication Data
We've Got Next: Herstory in History
Gina M. Stewart
p. cm

ISBN 978-1-939774-20-0 (pbk. :alk. Paper)

Religious life. 2. Conduct of life. 3. Christian Education.
Stewart, Gina M.

Printed in the U.S.A.

IN MEMORY
OF

My Daddy—Lepolia Stewart
October 8, 1935–March 9, 2007
Who said "If they don't elect her at the church,
I will build her a church"

My Friend and Mentor—Pastor Shirley Prince
Dec. 14, 1948–September 16, 2006
Your influence and imprint upon my life is undeniable

My Great Aunt—Oneather Mason
April 30, 1930–August 26, 2015
Who told everybody my story and said "the best is yet to come"

DEDICATION

To Rev. Eddie L. Currie-Pastor, Predecessor, Spiritual Father, and
Mentor who first believed that I had a story to tell

To All of the Preaching Women
whose voice(s) helped me to find my voice

To ALL of my "Preaching Sisters and Daughters"
"Carry out the Ministry God Has Given You"

CONTENTS

WORDS OF THANKSGIVING

In every thing give thanks: for this is the will of God in Christ
Jesus concerning you.

— 1 THESSALONIANS 5:18

MY LIFE AND PREACHING JOURNEY OVER THE PAST 25 YEARS
has been influenced by many people. I am compelled to give
appropriate thanks, not merely as a courtesy; but from the bottom of my heart. I would like to acknowledge some of the individuals who have been instrumental in my life and ministry.

I must first acknowledge my parents, Ann and the late Lepolia Stewart whose loving care and nurture created a wonderful environment for my personal and spiritual formation. I am
indebted to you for your unequivocal support that exemplified
a pure sense of selfless sacrifice for the betterment of my life. To
my maternal grandparents, the late Leroy and Odie Prewitt, I
owe a debt of gratitude for unconditional love that continues
to undergird my life to this day. Their daily practice of generosity cultivated a desire within me for a lifestyle of giving. I
am also grateful for the unparalleled support and daily doses
of encouragement that I receive from my siblings (Maria and
Dwight), sister-in-love Ann, extended family and network of
friends. You are the "wind beneath my wings."

I can't say enough about the late Rev. Eddie L. Currie, my
former pastor, predecessor and first mentor whose "hand" and
"blessing" upon my life was pivotal to my formation as a person
and preacher.

Thanks to every pastor, male and female (too numerous to name) who opened doors of opportunity and gave me a chance to "practice preaching" for your revivals, conferences and worship services. I give thanks to God every time I remember you.

I am grateful for the seminary communities of the Samuel DeWitt Proctor School of Theology of Virginia Union University and United Theological Seminary. My life has been enriched by the dialogue and interaction with students and faculty. Thank you Dr. John Kinney and Dr. Harold A. Hudson for your support and confidence.

Thank you Dr. David Emmanuel Goatley and the Lott Carey Foreign Mission Convention for your confidence in my ability to serve and for amplifying my global voice.

Thank you Women in Ministry Conference and Samuel DeWitt Proctor Conference for the privilege to partner in work and witness.

I am strengthened and sustained by a unique and gifted "band" of preaching women and their spouses Rev. Drs. Cynthia L. Hale, Elaine M. Flake (Dr. Floyd), Claudette A. Copeland (Bishop David), Jessica Kendall Ingram (Bishop Gregory), JoAnn Browning (Dr. Granger), Renita J. Weems (Rev. Martin), Carolyn A. Knight, Julia McMillan (Pastor Terry), Cheryl J. Sanders, Janet Floyd, Co-Pastor Dianne Young (Bishop William), and Bishop Carolyn Showell whose prayers, warm embrace, encouragement, wisdom and affirmation is a source of continual refreshment.

I am thankful to my "little big" brother, Rev. Dr. William H. Curtis for the invitation to serve as your Co-Mentor for the Curtis-Stewart D.Min. group at United Theological Seminary. I am sharpened by your intellect and inspired by your amazing gift for proclamation. Thank you Curtis-Stewart Fellows for your support.

Thank you Rev. Carla J. Howlett for telling my story to Rev. Martin Espinosa who told his wife Rev. Dr. Renita J. Weems that I had a story to tell. The rest really is history!

Thank you Dr. Walter Malone who continues to tell others that I have a story to tell. Your influence has opened many doors for which I am grateful.

Thank you Dr. Frank "Anthony" Thomas (Joyce) for your priestly ministry, encouragement and friendship.

Thank you Dr. Cat Stout for your gentle prodding and encouragement to publish. I love you and I am proud of you!

Thank you Danny Ray Thomas for your vision of "The Quiet Hour Team" and your advocacy. You have always been a tireless advocate for women. You were one of the first to say "you need to be heard." I am forever grateful to you.

I owe a debt of gratitude to every congregation and conference audience who heard any of these sermons that helped to refine them.

To the faithful staff, Associate Pastors, Ministry Directors, ministry assistants, deacons, intercessors and volunteer servants at Christ MB Church. You are such a gift to my life. Expect a harvest for your selfless sacrifice on my behalf. Thank you for "holding up my arms and lightening the load so that the burden of ministry is not so overwhelming. I give God praise for putting "my spirit" in and on you. Thank you Pastor Chuck, Minister Jeralyn and Stacy Shun, Phyllis, Jackie, Alicia, Adrian, Deacons Minnie, Ruby, Chris, and Linda, Collins, Anthony, and Edgar, Ministers Mona, BeBe, Terence, and Alfred (the SHIELD Ministry) for taking care of me so that I can take care of God's people.

I am grateful to the Christ Missionary Baptist Church in Memphis, Tennessee which was my incubator for preparation before they gave me the chance to serve as their pastor. Your pioneering witness and courageous example set a precedent for congregations across this nation and gave me a story worth telling. Your never-ending love, support and patience are a "life-giving" force.

Thank you Darryl Sims and MMGI Publishing for your persistence and patience in producing this work. You are a miracle worker!

Finally, I am grateful to the God who knew in my mother's womb that I would be a preacher! Thank you Lord for making me female and a Preacher! I offer this book as a first-fruit of "his/her" calling upon my life.

Soli Deo Gloria!

FOREWORD

ONE OF THE REWARDS OF ELEVATION IN ONE'S PROFESSION, especially if you're a woman in a male dominated profession, is that you get to distance yourself from labels, especially gendered labels. Professional recognition transforms you into a preacher, and not just a woman preacher. Clergy, not just a clergywoman. Writer, not just woman writer. Actor, not just an actress. Doctor, not a doctress. You preach sermons about women in the bible in that first half of your career, so that once you gain traction in the profession you won't ever have to preach sermons about women in the bible anymore in the second half of your career. But Rev. Dr. Gina Stewart is not interested in distancing herself from stories of women in the bible. Her aim in bringing together these life-changing sermons about women in the bible is to make it clear to all that she is not business-as-usual preacher. Preaching is about liberation for "Rev. Dr. Gina" as she is affectionately called by friends. Anyone who has ever heard this great preacher and interpreter of Scripture it's clear that she doesn't stand in the pulpit to razzle, dazzle, and wow her audience with her homilectical wizardry. Preaching is praxis for Rev. Dr. Gina, the praxis of preaching herstory. Drawing on the rich, but overlooked stories of women in the bible each sermon is a proclamation that God has in the past and continues in the present to use faithful, bold, courageous women to (re)write the narrative of divine redemption. Rev. Dr. Stewart demonstrates in her probing, prescient, power-ful, preaching that she is reclaiming the stories of oppressed, marginalized, nameless women in Scripture as part and parcel to her prophetical call to bring the good news of the gospel to oppressed, marginalized, hurting people living today. "Studying the women of the Bible is a necessary and much-needed activity," says Lisa Wilson Davison in her book, *Preaching the Women of the Bible*. "It is the only way to right the wrongs of sexist interpretations of the Bible and the resulting oppression of women."

If women in the pulpit don't bring fresh eyes and ears and voices to preaching, what is the point of our burgeoning numbers in the pulpit in the latter half of the 20th century and the first half of the 21st century? Preaching for Rev. Dr. Stewart is not about supplanting the stories of Abraham, Moses, David, Jeremiah, and Paul. Preaching herstory is about making sure his/story which we have is fuller and more complete by making certain women's contributions are not left out. Stories about women in the Bible indeed are not the only stories that need to be reframed and reexamined. Indeed, the entire cultural and narrative patriarchal framework of scripture deserves hyperscrutiny and reimagining by all of us whose job it is to wrestle the good news of the kingdom of God from hypermasculinized, male-centered texts. The Bible continues to be used to rationalize women's battery, invisibility, marginalization, oppression, and second-half status to men. Rescuing, reimagining, and reframing stories about the women in the Bible must be seen as part of the ongoing task of us who have studied and mastered the master's tools in the seminaries and divinity schools from which we graduated. In liberating their stories from the periphery and placing them front and center, we set the stage for our liberation to be agents of God's power and transformation today.

I am proud to be asked by my friend Rev. Dr. Gina to write the foreword to *We've Got Next: Herstory in History* because there is still a need for women's stories and a need for testimonies by women of how God uses little known, unnamed, marginalized, overlooked, ordinary people to disrupt the status quo. The day may come when it won't be a big deal that this is a book of sermons about women in the bible. The day may come when it won't be a big deal that this is a book of women's sermons by a woman preacher. But that day is not here. As long we can still turn on the news and hear about violence, abuse, brutality, and neglect of women, we will still need to hear Herstory, namely that God can and does use women to change and transform the world and to correct his/story.

Renita J. Weems, Ph.D.

INTRODUCTION

SEVERAL YEARS AGO, DR. RENITA J. WEEMS LED A PLENARY session for the *Women in Ministry* Conference in Atlanta, Georgia. In that session, she made a compelling case for the inclusion of women's stories in history with a particular emphasis on the importance of telling women's stories in our proclamation. Dr. Weems stated "Will our history as women in ministry and the church—this phenomenon in the latter half of the 20th century and here at the beginning of the 21st century that has swept the church marked by lots of Christian women's conferences and retreats—will it be recorded as business as usual or where we failed to move the needle by transforming this moment in history thus allowing history once more to overshadow herstory."

She challenged us as women preachers and pastors to "push the envelope" by giving careful attention to women not just on Women's Days but in our varied preaching opportunities. As I searched my personal mental rolodex to retrieve the sermons that I had heard and preached over the years, I found it true that women's voices were often not included in the conversation. Even more painful was my own admission that as a woman pastor, preacher and evangelist my preaching to some degree lacked intentionality in lifting up the voices and experiences of women.

That is precisely why this is a book of sermons about Women. It is not the first nor the last book of sermons about women that will be written. In fact there have been many sermons about women published by many outstanding preachers, pastors, and scholars. This book is simply this writer's attempt to be a faithful steward of *herstory* in history.

Herstory is still worth telling. At the time of this writing, many of our cities in America are potential powder kegs waiting to explode because of the senseless killing of Black men without weapons by law enforcement. It seems that everyday, there's a new hashtag with a new name of the latest victim trending on social media-#mikebrown, #freddiegray, #trayvonmartin, #tamirrice, #ericgarner, #walterscott and so many others. Equally as tragic are the nameless Black women who have lost their lives due to excessive force and racial profiling in policing. As thousands march and protest for justice, the names of the women killed by police—particularly women of color killed by police—continue to be less known.

In an effort to highlight the challenges Black women black women and girls face, the African American Policy Forum coauthored a policy brief and launched a social media campaign titled "Say Her Name." The effort aims to amplify the stories of African American women and girls who have been victims of police violence. The #Say Her Name campaign seeks to uplift the lives and experiences of black women killed by police and the many other forms of police violence black women experience" Women like #sandybland, #natashamckenna, #tanishanaderson, #yvettesmith, #darnishaharris and so many others.

In a Huffington Post article, activist Dream Hampton stated "The reason why it's important to center girls and women in this conversation is because the other narrative, and it's not a competing narrative, but it's just not a complete narrative, is that this only happens to black boys and men." The more complete narrative must be told. And if we don't tell it who will?

Unnamed women are not limited to BlackLivesMatter movements. There are unnamed women in the scripture and our contemporary world as well. The women and girls who are held captive by sex trafficking, women who struggle to survive and provide for their families, the women who suffer in silence because of domestic and sexual abuse, and even the Nigerian girls held hostage by Islamic extremists.

Although their names are often not mentioned, they do have names. Though often omitted in the pages of history and scripture their names are known to the God who was in Christ reconciling the world. We honor them when we tell their stories.

Herstory is not a *competing* narrative, but an attempt to complete the narrative. While women of the bible were restricted by ancient culture, patriarchy and invisibility, it is refreshing to discover the faithful, courageous, brave, and bold women of the Bible who speak through the centuries to confirm our calling, guide our lives, challenge our inertia and encourage our hearts.

It is my prayer that through these sermons, you will find that God spoke, intervened, challenged, transformed lives, brought healing and changed the narrative of redemption because of the word, work and witness of women. Courageous women like Esther and Shiprah and Puah, Risk-taking Women like Joanna and the Woman with the issue of blood, Faith-filled women like the Canaanite Woman, Liberated women like Leah and the Woman with the Bent Back. Profoundly patient women like Elizabeth, Generous Women like the woman with the Alabaster Jar and the Women at the tomb who were commissioned to proclaim a message of hope in world hostile to the gospel.

This book is not intended to be an exhaustive study of women in the bible. It is a compilation of several years of intentional preaching on women whose experiences inform our lives. May these sermons in this collection serve as proof that our lives and our stories matter.

Gina M. Stewart, D.Min.
Ordinary Time
August 2015

CHAPTER I

AN UNCOMPROMISED COMMITMENT

The king of Egypt said to the Hebrew midwives, whose names were Shiphrah and Puah, "When you are helping the Hebrew women during childbirth on the delivery stool, if you see that the baby is a boy, kill him; but if it is a girl, let her live." The midwives, however, feared God and did not do what the king of Egypt had told them to do; they let the boys live. Then the king of Egypt summoned the midwives and asked them, "Why have you done this? Why have you let the boys live?"

The midwives answered Pharaoh, "Hebrew women are not like Egyptian women; they are vigorous and give birth before the midwives arrive."

So God was kind to the midwives and the people increased and became even more numerous. And because the midwives feared God, he gave them families of their own.

Then Pharaoh gave this order to all his people: "Every Hebrew boy that is born you must throw into the Nile, but let every girl live."

—Exodus 1:15-22, NIV

WHEN WOMEN APPEAR IN THE BIBLE, THEY ARE OFTEN among the extras in the story. Sometimes they have supporting roles, but very rarely are they the stars. Like extras in a movie, even when they are the topic of discussion, they are often in the background.

This is because the stories of the Bible often reflect what theologian Lisa Wilson Davidson calls a "patriarchal, patrilineal and patrilocal society."[1] This means in practical and societal terms the culture is dominated by men, wives live with husbands' families, and land is passed down through male heirs.

The larger implication is that in the biblical text most of the primary concerns are male concerns. The storyline revolves around men. Even when women appear in the story, they are most often presented from a man's perspective. Thus while holding the belief that all scripture is given by inspiration of God, it cannot be denied that the Bible is a male production.

This is not just true for the Bible but it is true in society. In her book *Lean In*, Sheryl Sandberg states, "The blunt truth is that men still run the world. Despite significant strides made by women over the years, women often lag behind their male counterparts in most arenas of leadership and in compensation. And James Brown put it this way, it's a man's world."[2]

That is why I am struck by the story of Shiphrah and Puah. Their story is found in the Book of Exodus, a book which is dominated by men, like Moses, Pharaoh, Aaron, and Joshua. Ironically, there would be no Exodus from Egypt without the actions of five women. Jochebed, the mother of Moses, Miriam, Moses' sister, and Bithiah, Pharaoh's daughter, conspire to save and protect the life of Moses, the future liberator. But before Jochebed, Miriam, and Bithiah, there were two midwives, Shiphrah and Puah. They were not household names; they were marginal and peripheral characters; they were not persons of influence or affluence; they had no impressive pedigree; they had no imperial political power. In fact, by the estimations of their establishment, they were probably considered weak, impotent, and invisible. And yet there would have been no Exodus from Egypt had it not been for these women.

Shiphrah and Puah had a decision to make. Their orders were clear: all of the baby boys from among the Hebrews had to die. Their orders were murder. Pharaoh had said so. The

Pharaoh had said that any boy born to any Hebrew mother was to be put to death right there on the birthing stool. Before a male child's life could be lost to genocide, Pharaoh attempted to enlist these women to commit infanticide.

It was a defining moment in history. A change in the political structure had taken place and a new administration that did not know Joseph or his brothers was in charge. This Pharaoh had no commitment or loyalty to prior agreements made by his predecessor. Privileges granted by the previous administration no longer existed, had been forfeited or withdrawn.

Nevertheless, this small but favored nation of Hebrews was poised for liberation. Although they were slaves, they had preferred status because they had been chosen by God to receive the promises of God. But this favored status made them a threat to the empire. Although these people had done nothing wrong and there were no indications of conspiracy, their growth in number created fear, worry, and paranoia in the heart of the Pharaoh. The threat of the loss of control caused him to speculate that the Hebrew boys would grow up to be too strong and rise up against him, and he anticipated a potential exodus of a cheap labor source. So out of his anxiety Pharaoh generated a fresh policy of forced labor. Whips were cracked and commands were barked, with Hebrews bending over bricks for building and bending over fields for planting. Bent backs were intended to decrease the expanding number of Hebrews, but the plan backfired. Despite the forced labor, despite the unreasonable expectation to make bricks without straw with low and no wages, the Hebrews continued to multiply.

But Pharaoh would not be defeated. He tried to enlist the aid of Shiphrah and Puah, ordinary, marginal women. Midwives were extras in the larger scheme of things. They were to be seen and not heard. It was their job to deliver babies. But their boss, Pharaoh, wanted them to kill baby boys because he was no friend to the Israelites and he feared the Israelites.

Because Pharaoh feared the Israelites, he did what fearful and insecure leaders sometimes do: he created policies to oppress them, and he created an enemy where there was none. He stirred up his people to fear the Israelites.

As we observe so often in life, the oppressor "fears" the oppressed. Oppressors tend to fear the oppressed. From Selma to Memphis, from Ferguson to New York, from Libya to South Africa, from Israel to America, the oppressor always fears the oppressed.

The question that is always on the mind of the oppressor is, What will the oppressed do if they become too many and they have access to power? What will the rich do if the poor want more? What will the women do if they are allowed to share in leadership? What will immigrants do if they are granted the privilege of citizenship? The oppressor tends to fear the oppressed. Pharaoh was no exception. He too, feared the oppressed So Pharaoh issued an order and he said to the midwives: "When you help the Hebrew women in childbirth and observe them on the delivery stool, if it is a boy, kill him; but if it is a girl, let her live."[3]

But the text says, "The midwives, however, feared God and did not do what the king of Egypt had told them to do; they let the boys live."[4] The Message translation says: "But the midwives had far too much respect for God and didn't do what the king of Egypt ordered." In other words, in the final analysis, because the midwives worked for God, they would not carry out Pharaoh's plan. Even though Pharaoh had the power and the authority according to the law to put them to death, God was the final authority for Shiphrah and Puah. And because Shiphrah and Puah worked for God, they told Pharaoh no. They said no to evil. They chose liberation over capitalism. They sought vigilance over violence. They exercised discipline over destruction.

And their action put them at great risk. Pharaoh was the most powerful man in the land and had shown a willingness to kill whoever got in his way. Pharaoh could do whatever he wanted to whomever he wanted. Pharaoh built pyramids. Pharaoh controlled the known world. Pharaoh enslaved people. Pharaoh was rich beyond imagination. In fact, at that time Pharaoh was perceived as a god– a little g.o.d. People bowed down to old Pharaoh, and they did what he said. People feared Pharaoh.

But because the midwives feared God and they had respect for God, their act of defiance/resistance is perhaps history's first recorded act of civil disobedience. These two women, at great peril to themselves, disobeyed Pharaoh's orders because Pharaoh's authority was in direct contradiction to God's authority. And for these two women, this amounted to irreconcilable differences. At great risk to themselves, they claimed their moral authority.

When Pharaoh confronted them, they expressed to Pharaoh what was true about the women: they said that the Hebrew women are vigorous and strong and they give birth before the midwives arrive. Although Shiphrah and Puah have been taken to task for "telling a lie," Shiphrah "uses the age-old technique in which the weak have survived in the midst of the strong. Deception, hypocrisy, lying become the mechanism by which the weak protect themselves from the strong."[5] So even though their actions put them at risk, Shiphrah and Puah were in touch with their God-given vocation.

Pharaoh didn't understand what he was asking the women to do because he was operating out of an *imagined threat* to Egyptian national security and self-preservation. But the midwives were operating out of a moral commitment. They remained true to their vocation or their calling. They understood that their primary vocation was grounded on the hope of assisting in bringing forth life rather than death.

Scholars tell us that midwives in Israel were barren women. In a culture where having children and a family was the ordinary way to build a life to gain respect, to know the blessing of

God these barren, somewhat marginal women found their place in the community by helping other women bring forth new life. Their daily work, their daily routine, what they got up in the morning to do, was to help to bring new life into the world.

Is that not what midwives do? They don't stand on the sidelines. They show up, they attend, they listen, they encourage, they coach, they stay as long as they are needed. They roll up their sleeves and get involved in bringing new life into the world. In doing so, they are exposed to all sorts of things: stillbirths, painful births, poverty, pain, cruelty, suffering, compassion, joy, heroism, and injustice.

And we have the same opportunity. We don't have to work in the delivery room to qualify as a midwife. We act as a midwife whenever we roll up our sleeves and get involved in bringing new life into the world. We act as a midwife whenever we step off the sidelines and enter into the thick of the joy and pain of the world. When we see something happening that is unjust and we speak up we are acting as a midwife.

Every time we tutor a child, whenever we address literacy to help students qualify for college exams, we're acting as a midwife. When we mentor teenage boys and girls, we're acting as a midwife. When we host a workshop, we're acting as a midwife. Whenever we address domestic violence, we're acting as a midwife. Whenever we address hunger or HIV/AIDS, we're acting as a midwife.

Whenever we address social injustices, inequality, voter information, voter fraud, and registration, we're acting as a midwife. Whenever we assist the poor and under- represented, whenever we provide access to food, clothing, shelter, job opportunities, and many more needs of the community, we're acting as a midwife.

When we choose to stand with the oppressed and marginalized, we are acting as a midwife. Whenever we take to the streets or lift our voices in protest, we're acting as a midwife. Whenever we look into the eyes of those who are considered expendable and see a life worth saving, we are acting as a midwife. When we act as our brother's and sister's keeper in word and in deed, we're acting as a midwife.

Thank God for a history that reminds us of the midwives who brought new life to women and men around the world in times of racial, economic, and gender inequality. Thank God for Freedmen's Bureaus and historically black colleges and universities. Thank God for the Student Nonviolent Coordinating Committee, for the Southern Christian Leadership Conference, for Rainbow Push-People United to Save Humanity, for the NAACP, for the Civil Rights Movement. Thank God for Black sororities and fraternities and Greek letter organizations and other agencies, seminaries, and organizations committed to the uplift of other human beings.

Thank God for midwives who were called to political and social action, for those who pooled their collective strength to promote equality, support the under-served, educate and stimulate participation in the establishment of positive public policy, promote academic excellence, and provide solutions for problems in their communities. Thank God for the midwives who would not keep silent in the face of oppression and suppression of women but who participated in the Women's Suffrage march in Washington D.C., who marched on the state capitol, and who marched on the Edmund Pettus Bridge. Thank God for those who marched in Memphis to bring dignity to the sanitation workers.

Thank God for the midwives. Thank God for the midwives who used their power to resist the advancement of evil, discrimination, and oppression. Thank God for the midwives who possessed an uncompromising commitment to participate in God's liberating work.

And here is why we thank God for the midwives and why we still need midwives: because Pharaoh is not dead. For you see, Pharaoh is not just a person. Pharaoh is an institution. Pharaoh is any institution or person who controls our lives.

Pharaoh is anyone or anything that stands in the way of our claiming our high calling from God.

There are so many equations that compete to shape our behavior as a society, as women and men, as professionals, and yes even as scholars and pastors and preachers and people of faith. If we're not careful, we can become vulnerable, complicit, and susceptible to pressures to conform to the wrong values, to give in to power even when that power is used for destructive or evil purposes, to live a lie, and to deny our calling. When we're called to be helpers, we turn into hurters because power told us to.

Ah, but we who fear the Lord know that God still works through the hands of midwives. We serve the God who still sees and hears the cries of babies in baskets in the bulrushes. We serve the God who still sees and hears the cries of the marginalized and the oppressed. We serve a God who still hears the cries of at-risk children. We serve a God who still hears the cries of heartbroken mothers who grieve the loss of sons and daughters. We serve a God who still hears the cries of the unemployed and the invisible.

And we believe in a God who still works in mysterious ways, who works through the secretive ways of prostitutes who hide Jewish spies, the unexpected faithfulness of foreigners like Ruth, the riskiness of Mary, "Handmaid of the Lord," and the courage of midwives.

And it is because of their courage and uncompromised commitment that an entire narrative for a nation was changed. For if they had not said no to killing Moses, the Exodus narrative would have been quite different. Although Moses, Isaac, Joshua, and Caleb get top billing in the scriptures for what they did, the entire book of Exodus hinges on what these midwives did.

Because the midwives feared God, they saved the lives of babies including Moses the great deliverer. And because of their courage and conviction and uncompromised commitment slaves could imagine a different reality. So keep on keep on asserting your moral authority, keep on lobbying, keep on protesting injustice, keep on touching lives around the world. Because when you do, you walk in the tradition of Moses, Miriam, Esther, Deborah, Joshua, Mary Church Terrell, Shirley Chisholm, Betty Shabazz, Barbara Jordan, Mary McLeod Bethune, Melissa Harris-Perry, Dr. Dorothy Height, Winnie Mandela, Rev. Traci Blackmon, and Jesus!

Because that is how God works! It is not always in the power of the ways of the world. God is most alive in the back rooms of midwives delivering life into places of death and slavery and oppression and hopelessness. God is most present in those places of discerned absence and God still does some of God's best work through midwives like Shiphrah and Puah, midwives with an uncompromised commitment.

Notes

1. Lisa Wilson Davidson, *Preaching the Women of the Bible* (Kindle Version, 2006), 4.10.

2. Sheryl Sandberg, *Lean In: Women, Work, and the Will to Lead* (New York: Knopf, 2013).

3. Exodus 1:16, NIV.

4. Exodus 1:17, NIV.

5. Howard Thurman, *Deep River and The Negro Spiritual Speaks of Life and Death* (Richmond: Friends United Press, 1975). 44–45.

CHAPTER 2

THE FIERCE URGENCY OF NOW

On a Sabbath Jesus was teaching in one of the synagogues, and a woman was there who had been crippled by a spirit for eighteen years. She was bent over and could not straighten up at all. When Jesus saw her, he called her forward and said to her, "Woman, you are set free from your infirmity." Then he put his hands on her, and immediately she straightened up and praised God.

Indignant because Jesus had healed on the Sabbath, the synagogue leader said to the people, "There are six days for work. So come and be healed on those days, not on the Sabbath."

The Lord answered him, "You hypocrites! Doesn't each of you on the Sabbath untie your ox or donkey from the stall and lead it out to give it water? Then should not this woman, a daughter of Abraham, whom Satan has kept bound for eighteen long years, be set free on the Sabbath day from what bound her?"

When he said this, all his opponents were humiliated, but the people were delighted with all the wonderful things he was doing.

—Luke 13:10-17, NIV

July 4, 1776 was the day that the colonies decided to declare themselves independent of Britain. By writing a very detailed decree, they decided that they no longer would need to be governed by the kings of England who had been so very unjust to the colonists in the years before, and on July 4th, America was born.

What is ironic is that from a historical perspective while America was declaring and claiming its independence from Great Britain, 100 years earlier around the 16th century, Africans were brought to American shores as slaves and were not freed until Lincoln signed the Emancipation Proclamation in 1863, and even after it was signed into law, Jim Crow laws were created to deny African Americans the benefits of their full emancipation.

It's a strange irony that one group would seek to liberate itself from another while at the same time hold another group hostage to the same principle it seeks to be liberated or freed from. This raises other interesting questions. Questions like, Why do the oppressed oppress others? How do the oppressed out-oppress the oppressor? Why do some Blacks who have been marginalized, disenfranchised, and oppressed oppress women and children? Why do women who have been oppressed, looked-over, locked-out, left-out, and tolerated rather than celebrated oppress other women? Why do those who were once outsiders become insiders and then turn around and oppress the outsiders when they become insiders? Why do older members oppress new members and then when new members become old members, the new old members turn around and oppress the newer members? Why do older folks oppress younger folks? Why do we make rules that we break and then turn around and demand others to follow rules that we openly break?

It is this kind of hypocrisy and inconsistency that Jesus addresses in this preaching passage.

This is a story about a delivered woman. Jesus has just set her free from an infirmity that has had her bound for eighteen years. Because of her physical condition, the text does not say anything is wrong with her mind, but because of her physical condition, for eighteen years, this woman has been excluded from the privileges of being human. She is already marginalized because of her gender, but her condition also contributed to her marginalization.

Luke the physician describes her as a woman with a spirit of infirmity. She was woman with a spirit of weakness or impotence, or powerlessness.

In this instance, Satan stands behind the affliction of this woman. She had been crippled for eighteen years and was not in a position to lift herself up. The text says that it was because of the devil that she had been bound for eighteen years. And while the devil may not be behind all suffering, the devil is not innocent when it comes to suffering.

For eighteen years, she had been staring at the floor. For eighteen years, she couldn't look out the window. For eighteen years, she was unable to stand, sit, or even lie down in bed. For eighteen years, she couldn't straighten her crooked back. This unidentified woman had been in bondage to an infirmity/weakness that had crippled her and kept her in a state of impotence and powerlessness for eighteen years.

The text provides no specifics about the root biomedical cause of this woman's stooped posture—a crooked spine, osteoporosis, arthritis, etc. The text doesn't tell us, but we can be sure that she suffered from chronic unrelenting pain as a result.

No doubt the pain must have been debilitating, limiting, and stressful. And for sure, a cure or healing to someone in her condition would no doubt be and feel like a form of liberation.

But even though she is stooped over, something is to be said for her commitment to be in worship after eighteen years. If I had been crippled for eighteen years, I wonder if I would be faithful to still worship God after being in the same condition for eighteen years. Longevity in suffering has a way of testing the depth of our faith and our commitment.

Most of us can handle short-term disappointments, sicknesses, setbacks, interruptions, and abandonment, but long-term disappointments, sicknesses, setbacks, interruptions, and abandonment have a way of testing the depth of our commitment and resilience. It's not as difficult to maintain a consistent level of commitment and loyalty to God when things are going according to our schedule or plan, but long-term disappointment and disorientation have a way of testing out the depth of our commitment. There is something to be said for this woman who is found in worship after suffering for eighteen years.

And the text doesn't say it, but I have a sneaky suspicion that this is not the first time this woman has come looking for divine help. I have a suspicion that this woman had probably prayed and asked God for help, and yet she was not delivered.

But it was on this particular day that heaven has come down to the synagogue. For it was on this particular day Jesus was teaching in the synagogue on the Sabbath. God incarnate, the Word made flesh, truth personified, *Jesus of Nazareth* was teaching in the synagogue. The Jesus who had compassion for the people. The Jesus whom the common people heard gladly. The Jesus who was willing to risk reputation and social contamination by holding a conversation with a woman at the well in broad daylight. The Jesus who forgave a woman caught in the very act of adultery. The Jesus who stood up the woman with the alabaster jar and said, "leave her alone!"

It was Jesus of Nazareth (who with radar sensitivity and compassion) sees this dejected, disabled, diminished, demoralized, disenfranchised, debilitated, downcast woman. It was on this particular day in the synagogue that Jesus calls her forward and addresses the woman. Jesus initiates the healing, "summoning" her, speaking life to her, saying, "Woman, be loosed from your sickness," and when Jesus put his hands on her, she immediately straightened up and praised God. When she couldn't act for herself, Jesus took the initiative, broke her isolation, and brought her back into community. Jesus sees saw her, speaks to her, lays hands on her, and said says to her, "Woman though art loosed from thine infirmity. Woman, you are released, set free, no longer detained by what cripples you, no longer detained by the crippling condition. You are free from your weakness."

Jesus lifts her from shame to a place of honor. And even though Satan had had her bound—because Satan does bow people down, but so does sin, sorrow, and suffering—Jesus is the only One who can set the captive free. He spoke the word, laid His hands on her, and she was healed. A divine reversal takes place and the woman was immediately made straight and she began to glorify God, which is appropriate when you come in contact with God's grace, for the proof of the woman's restoration is immediate. She is immediately able to stand straight and glorify God, which is the only appropriate response to God's redemptive power. That was a synagogue service the people never forgot. It was a day that a woman received her liberation.

But here is the paradox: her liberation led to indignation. The text says that the leader of the synagogue was indignant because Jesus healed on the Sabbath. Instead of rejoicing and glorifying God as they witnessed the manifestation of the glory of God right before their eyes, the ruler of the synagogue (see Luke 8:41) became very angry. You would think that the leader of the community of faith would be celebrating with the woman!

But the ruler of the synagogue challenged Jesus. And the ruler of the synagogue said, "There are six days on which it is necessary to work, so come on those days to be healed, and not on the Sabbath day." Note that it was acceptable to come to the synagogue to worship but don't come to be healed.

Contemporary readers are hard-pressed to understand why the synagogue leaders would express such indignation with this woman's liberation. Why wouldn't they celebrate this woman's deliverance! Eighteen years is a long time. It's long time to be sick, it's long time to be unemployed, it's a long time to be isolated. Eighteen years is a long time!

And the synagogue ruler says, "We don't heal on the Sabbath." This reminds me of some of the meetings that we have, in the name of God, for the sake of God, but we don't necessarily want a real move of God. The implication is "don't break the rules." Sometimes we allow our pursuit of religious practices to outweigh our responsibility to be compassionate. The synagogue leader responds with indignation because the Sabbath was not the right day for healing.

Although what the synagogue ruler said is important to the story, why he said it is even more important to the story. For you see, his indignation was a matter of interpretation. The attitude of the ruler of the synagogue was informed by their *interpretation* of the law—that one should deliberately avoid treating non-fatal wounds and injuries on the Sabbath. In other words, it was permissible to treat what was considered critical but not chronic, meaning it was permissible to treat if her condition had involved immediate danger or death, but not chronic—long-term or frequent.

The ruler's attitude was that this woman's condition was chronic and not critical. Her situation did not have the urgency of something like childbirth, a heart attack, or a stroke. It was much closer to the case of a broken limb or a dislocated foot. So because the woman's condition was chronic, but not critical, in the ruler's mind, one more day wouldn't make a difference. Jesus and her healing could have waited one more day. It would have been better to wait another day rather than violate the Sabbath.

I find it amazing how there is always someone who wants to say that one more day won't kill you. They don't live with our realities, bear our pain, or share our struggles, but they say, "One more day won't kill you."

Although the leader of the synagogue's indignation is due to his concern for proper observance of Sabbath rather than celebration of the woman's release from her condition, Jesus responds to his indignation about her liberation with a word of vindication; he clears her name. Jesus says, "You hypocrites, doesn't each of you untie or loose his ox or donkey from the stall and lead it out to give it water? Then should not this woman, a daughter of Abraham whom Satan has kept bound for eighteen long years, be set free on the Sabbath day from what bound her?" In other words, Jesus is saying, "She ain't got to wait another day!"

Perhaps you are in the company of the chronic and not the critical. Critical means that it's urgent. Chronic implies that something has been going on for a long time. You've been depressed a long time, you have been frustrated a long time, you have been tired a long time, you have been disillusioned a long time, you have been waiting a long time, you have been praying a long time. You have been in a position of powerlessness, helplessness, defeat, impotence, etc., for so long that it has become normative for you.

There are some people and some of us who have been in situations and conditions for so long that we have accepted it as a way of life. But thank God that on that day in the synagogue Jesus made an urgent utterance because he understood the fierce urgency of now.

Some things just can't wait another eighteen years. The blood of women who have died in police custody without justice demands that we not wait another eighteen years. The release of the Nigerian school girls demands that we cannot wait another day. The women and girls who have been lured into human trafficking demand that we cannot wait another day.

People who have been wrongfully imprisoned don't have the luxury of waiting another day. People who can't feed their families can't wait another day. Women and children who are in need of health care can't wait another day. There are seniors who are on Medicaid who can't wait another day.

Perhaps you are one of them who can't wait another eighteen years, eighteen months, eighteen weeks, eighteen hours, or eighteen seconds. You need a breakthrough right now! And the reason why this is so important is because there will always be somebody who says, "Not yet." When Blacks were in slavery, the racial supremacists said, "Not yet." When Blacks were freed from slavery, Jim Crow said, "Not yet." When Blacks fought for the right to vote, somebody said, "Not yet."

When a black man from the south side of Chicago believed that he could be president of U.S., somebody said, "Not yet." When a woman felt a call to preach, there were some who said and still say, "Not yet." When the Christ M.B. Church in Memphis, Tennessee, was pondering electing a female as their pastor, somebody said, "Not yet." There will always be somebody who wants to say, "Not yet."

But thank God that Jesus declares that healing for this woman is "mission critical." Critical enough to break the rules. Critical enough to set her free on the Sabbath. Critical enough to release her from her infirmity.

There is something grossly hypocritical about treating animals better than we treat people. There's something grossly hypocritical when a bill can be drafted in response to the innocent loss of life of Cecil the Lion but we are still waiting for a verdict on the loss of innocent human lives. There's something grossly hypocritical when people can get in an uproar about abortion but think nothing of starving children after they born or depriving senior citizens of needed benefits when they reach old age. There's something grossly hypocritical when we can bomb abortion clinics in the name of God but have no regard for the sanctity of the lives of unarmed black women and men whose premature deaths were caused by violence and excessive force.

Jesus is saying that *anytime* is the right time to exercise the ministry of release from the bondage of Satan and anytime is the right time for a demonstration of God's compassion. Anytime is the right time to access the power of God. Anytime is the right time to access God's presence.

So go back to your churches, go back to your cities, go back to your jobs, go back to your families and tell somebody about the fierce urgency of now! The thief comes to kill, steal, and destroy, but Jesus says, "I have come that they may life and have it more abundantly—not next week, not next month, not next year, but right now!"

This is the message that we must keep on preaching and proclaiming—that oppression doesn't have to have the last word! Every day we come in contact with people who are bent over from trying to meet other's expectations, bent over from suffering, bent over from sin, bent over from sorrow, bent over by insecurity, bent over by shame, bent over because of marginalization, bent over by victimization, bent over by isolation, bent over from poverty, bent over from a broken justice system. There are some folks who don't have another eighteen years, eighteen months, eighteen days, eighteen minutes, or eighteen seconds. But we can announce that God has and is already acting on our behalf. Just as Jesus met that woman in the synagogue, I am so glad that Jesus is still meeting folks right where we are. The Lord will meet you where you are. He will speak to you, pronounce you restored, touch you, defend you against your opponents, and welcome you to be a part of the family of God.

Whatever the problem, whatever the challenge, whatever the situation, Jesus offers a deliverance that is designed to free us up to relate to him in a way that enables us to shed the limitations Satan sometimes seeks to chain us with. The establishing of a relationship with God and the access to the power of God's presence in God's Spirit empowers us with resources to renew our lives. Anytime is appropriate for such a move towards restoration. It is what Jesus' ministry—and the church's ministry today—are all about.

Jesus gave his life for our restoration. Your full restoration may not be all at once like the woman's restoration in this story. That may have to wait until we meet our God face-to-face. But this woman's healing is our clue that the reign of God's wholeness has begun, in the fierce urgency of now.

CHAPTER 3

A TRANSFORMED
NON-CONFORMIST

After this, Jesus traveled about from one town and village to another, proclaiming the good news of the kingdom of God. The Twelve were with him, and also some women who had been cured of evil spirits and diseases: Mary (called Magdalene) from whom seven demons had come out; Joanna the wife of Chuza, the manager of Herod's household; Susanna; and many others. These women were helping to support them out of their own means.

—LUKE 8:1-3, NIV

IN HIS BOOK *STRENGTH TO LOVE*, DR. MARTIN LUTHER King, Jr. says, "Do not conform is difficult advice in a generation when crowd pressures and peer influences have unconsciously conditioned our minds and feet to move to the rhythmic drumbeat of the status quo."[1] King states that many voices and forces urge us to choose the path of least resistance and bid us never to fight for an unpopular cause and never to be found in a pathetic minority of two or three. Further, he says, "Success, recognition and conformity are the bywords of our post-modern world where everyone seems to crave the anesthetizing security of being identified with the majority."[2]

It is not always easy or popular to march to the beat of a different drum. Those who make such noble attempts discover that those rare and courageous individuals who dare to

translate ideals into reality are often met with frustration, opposition, and sometimes defeat. Reform and change—as we
have witnessed with the election of the first African American president, the rise in tea party politics, deadlock debates,
ideological scrimmages, and increasing incivility—change and
progress often comes with a price.

We have proof from scripture and history that confirms
that those who choose to think and behave differently in the
pursuit of a more noble and just cause have paid a high price.
Some even paid for it with their lives.

In spite of the prevailing tendency to conform, believers
have a mandate to be non-conformists. As we are challenged
in Romans 12:2:"Do not conform to the pattern of this world,
but be transformed by the renewing of your mind." The J.B.
Phillips translation says:"Don't let the world squeeze you into
its mold, but let God re-mould your minds from within, so
that you may prove in practice that the plan of God for you is
good, meets all His demands and moves towards the goal of
true maturity."

Believers have a mandate to live differently and according to
a higher loyalty. We are called to be people of conviction, not
conformity. This is our eternal challenge as Christians.

While this is a noble and lofty aspiration, our rhetoric is
often more powerful than our practice. That is why I am particularly struck by the sister in our text. I believe that Dr. King
would describe her as a transformed non-conformist. She is
named along with Mary Magdalene, Susanna, and other unnamed women who followed Jesus and committed their financial resources to support the itinerant ministry of Jesus.

Her name is Joanna, the wife of Chuza, Herod's household
manager—the official over the financial interests of the emper-
or."Hardly anyone knows Joanna. Theologians in their studies
never meet her, and for the most part, she has been ignored in
biblical texts. She is only mentioned twice—in Luke 8 and Luke

24. She often does not appear in most books about women of the Bible and when she does, she is quickly passed over."[3]

What is the reason for this note about Joanna's life and contribution? Certainly brevity and anonymity in scripture do not necessarily equate to insignificance, for Joseph of Arimathea, those who "shoot dice" at the foot of the cross, the disciple who fled naked at Jesus' arrest, the woman with the issue of blood, the woman at the well, the widow of Nain, the woman with the lost coin, the thief on the cross, and even the mother of the sons of Zebedee are all mentioned with brevity or anonymity. And yet while they have stimulated the imagination, Joanna is hardly ever mentioned or preached about.

Joanna was a woman from court society, the wife of a senior royal official following Jesus. She was from the aristocracy, from the establishment. She was a woman of status, wealth, and influence; a woman with a secure life at the side of an influential government official who decides to share in the risky and penurious life of a popular radical, controversial, social revolutionary, Jesus.

Joanna was counted in the company of the women who traveled with and provided financial support to Jesus as he traveled. Joanna and her friends were not just groupies. They were women with a particular mission. They were not just spectators, but they were stakeholders. They followed Jesus and gave unselfishly of their substance to support Jesus' itinerant ministry.

Joanna, Mary, and Susanna were counted in the company with their own particular struggles, but they all shared a common story. The text says they had been healed by Jesus.[4] Healed of evil spirits and infirmities, demonic oppression, and possession. Once they were healed by Jesus they began to play a vital role in the healing process of others. They traveled with Jesus with a purpose and presence. They were a living exhibit of the power of Jesus. Their mere presence was a silent witness to the power and compassion of the Healer Himself. Each of them had come in contact with the power of God and they were never the same. Whatever their illness or infirmity was, their encounter with Jesus was an experience that dramatically impacted their lives. This is the testimony of these women who followed Jesus.

Dr. Samuel Proctor argues that although Mary Magdalene and Susanna are also mentioned in this group, Joanna demands more space and reflection because there are a great number of people in our churches and our culture who have been touched by the hand of Jesus but who would never dare to do what Joanna did. Joanna is significant because even though she was close to the political power structure in Palestine, even though her husband worked for the government, she chose to follow Jesus from town to town, celebrating the good news of the Kingdom of God and giving of her substance. Her husband worked in the enemy's camp, but Joanna's encounter with Jesus was so compelling and transformative that she risked a great deal just to be identified or associated with Jesus.

It must be noted that Joanna is the wife of Chuza, a manager of Herod's estate. And it is no secret how Herod felt about Jesus. This Herod is the son of Herod who had tried to kill the baby Jesus by slaughtering all two-year-olds around Bethlehem. This is Herod who imprisoned and beheaded John the Baptist. This is Herod Antipas who would later mock Jesus on the night he was arrested. Joanna's husband was on this Herod's payroll. But Joanna dared to step outside of her safe, secure, affluent comfort zone to follow Jesus.

No doubt, Joanna's encounter with Jesus ushered in a new season of her life. It was no longer business as usual. Joanna traveled with Jesus and used Herod's money to finance Jesus' ministry.

Joanna, a transformed non-conformist, used her wealth and influence and even risked her life to follow Jesus! Many of us—with good ideas, talent, creativity, gifts, graces, and anointing—could make a meaningful contribution toward the transformation of the culture and God's world if we were willing to abandon our neutrality and function as a transformed non-conformist. Many of us could change the world if we were not so timid about breaking ranks with friends, associates, colleagues, and church members who are enslaved to the status quo.

Joanna's courageous actions present a fitting challenge for all of us, for whom among has not been enticed by the cult of conformity or the pressure to conform? We see it in our children by their desire to fit in. We see it in the church as it has remained silent in the face of the immoral and the unethical. We see it in preachers who preach comforting sermons and avoid saying anything from the pulpit that will disturb the comfortable or comfort the disturbed. We see it in our own lives: the times that we have been silent when we should have spoken; the times when we have allowed the actions and thoughts of other individuals to produce conformity to a particular way of acting or thinking in our own lives even if it is wrong, immoral, or unethical.

Joanna's courageous decision to risk everything to follow Jesus is a reminder today that it really does take courage to follow Jesus of Nazareth, not just in word but also in deed. It takes courage to preach prophetically when all people want is a message about prosperity. It takes courage to minister to the left out, the locked out, and the overlooked. It takes courage to embrace an egalitarian mantle of leadership and free up women to serve alongside men. It took courage for Dr. King to go to Memphis to fight for sanitation workers. It took courage for Winnie Mandela to continue the fight against apartheid in South Africa after Nelson Mandela's arrest. It took courage for Richard Allen and Absalom Jones to walk out of a White Methodist church and form the AME church. It took courage for Rosa Parks to refuse to give up her seat. And it takes courage to follow Jesus of Nazareth in our contemporary world.

Joanna and these courageous women are our reminders today that that the rights of Black folk, women, men, and children,
have been won by courageous transformed non-conformists
like Ida B. Wells, Sojourner Truth, Shirley Chisholm, Mary
McLeod Bethune, Diane Nash, and Maxine Waters. And there
are other transformed non-conformists whose names never
made the headlines, but they were regular men and women bus
drivers, domestic workers, teachers, laborers, and professionals
who were courageous enough to be transformed non-conformists. They are our reminders that the salvation of God's world
still lies in the hands of transformed non-conformists like
Shadrach, Meshach, and Abednego, who when ordered to bow
before a golden image said in no uncertain terms, Do what you
have to do, throw us in the furnace if you want to, our God will
deliver us, but if he doesn't, we still won't bow to your golden
image. The salvation of the world lies in the hands of folks like
Daniel, who refused to stop praying even when he was thrown
into a lions' den. The salvation of the world lies in the hands
of men like 1st-century apostles who wouldn't shut up even
when their lives were threatened. The salvation of the world
lies in the hands of transformed non-conformists like Rahab,
who understood that the God of the Exodus was greater than
the God of Sihon and Og. The salvation of the world lies in the
hands of men and women who would dare to do what Joanna
and so many others did—count the cost and take up the cross
and follow Jesus!!! Authentic transformed non-conformists are
the men and women who are courageous enough to pay the
price, and are courageous enough to be identified with Jesus.

In fact, it was a transformed non-conformist who was born
in a manger in Bethlehem, who healed the sick and raised
Lazarus, who challenged the status quo, who spoke truth to
power, and who was tried and sentenced to a humiliating and
excruciating death, but in the face of extreme pressure he would
not compromise. He would not come down from the cross to

save himself. He decided to die to save you and me. Hallelujah! Amen!

NOTES

1. Martin Luther King Jr., *Strength to Love* (Minneapolis: Fortress Press Gift Edition, 2010), 11.

2. Ibid., 12.

3. Elisabeth Moltmann-Wendel, *The Women Around Jesus* (New York: J.R. Bowden, 1982), 133.

4. Luke 8:2.

CHAPTER 4

A RISK OF FAITH

After Jesus crossed over by boat, a large crowd met him at the seaside. One of the meeting-place leaders named Jairus came. When he saw Jesus, he fell to his knees, beside himself as he begged, "My dear daughter is at death's door. Come and lay hands on her so she will get well and live." Jesus went with him, the whole crowd tagging along, pushing and jostling him.

A woman who had suffered a condition of hemorrhaging for twelve years—a long succession of physicians had treated her, and treated her badly, taking all her money and leaving her worse off than before—had heard about Jesus. She slipped in from behind and touched his robe. She was thinking to herself, "If I can put a finger on his robe, I can get well." The moment she did it, the flow of blood dried up. She could feel the change and knew her plague was over and done with.

At the same moment, Jesus felt energy discharging from him. He turned around to the crowd and asked, "Who touched my robe?"

His disciples said, "What are you talking about? With this crowd pushing and jostling
you, you're asking, 'Who touched me?' Dozens have touched you!"
But he went on asking, looking around to see who had done it.
The woman, knowing
what had happened, knowing she was the one, stepped up in fear and trembling, knelt
before him, and gave him the whole story.

Jesus said to her, "Daughter, you took a risk of faith, and now you're healed and whole. Live well, live blessed! Be healed of your plague."

—MARK 5:21-34, THE MESSAGE

THANKS TO THE PERSISTENCE OF PRESIDENT OBAMA, THE Affordable Health Care Act (ACA) is now the law of the land despite the numerous attempts of die-hard opponents to repeal it. The ACA has provided health insurance to more than 12 million Americans through the federal exchange and millions more through Medicaid. And although there is room for improvement, we rejoice that millions of people now have access to healthcare despite pre-existing conditions.

However, as great as this news may be for some, in some states there are still some who will "fall through the cracks." Workers who earn below $11,670 for a single person and up to $46,680 for families cannot afford to purchase the healthcare. The 2010 health law was meant to cover people in these income brackets by expanding Medicaid for workers earning up to the federal poverty line to receive federal subsidies. But the Supreme Court in 2012 struck down the law's requirement that states expand their Medicaid coverage. This meant that states could decide to opt out of expanding Medicaid coverage.

Many elected officials in 24 states (my state Tennessee is one of them) declined the expansion, triggering a coverage gap. Officials said an expansion would add burdensome costs and, in some cases, leave more people dependent on government. This decision created a gap for millions of Americans at the lowest income levels who don't qualify for Medicaid coverage under varying state rules. Lower-income people in half the states get no help, while better-off workers elsewhere can buy insurance with taxpayer-funded subsidies.

It is a tragic commentary that America is increasingly becoming a place where people "fall through the cracks." The mentally ill "fall through the cracks," the poor "fall the through the cracks," the unemployed and underemployed "fall through the cracks," and women and children "fall through the cracks."

I have met people in Third-world countries who consider America to be The Promised Land. Some of them believe that everyone in America is rich, and by comparison that may appear to be so and is true in many cases, but the truth is that poverty is still a problem in America.

I am grateful that I live in America, a place where dreams can and do come true, but I must say that while the thought of having a chance or an opportunity sounds nice in theory—and in recent years has served as the basis for some of the most extreme budget reductions presented on the floor of Congress—opportunity does not always take into account that the playing field is not always level. It does not consider the realities of racism, sexism, classism, and poverty that lock and shut people out. And of course when we check the statistics, we find that we can't discuss poverty without including women in the discussion.

According to the Center for American Progress website, women in America are more likely to be poor than men. Over half of the 37 million Americans living in poverty today are women. And women in America are further behind than women in other countries—the gap in poverty rates between men and women is wider in America than anywhere else in the Western world. Consider the following facts:

+ Poverty rates are higher for women than men. In 2007, 13.8 percent of females were poor compared to 11.1 percent of men.
+ Women are poorer than men in all racial and ethnic groups.
+ Black and Latina women face particularly high rates of poverty. Black and Latina women are at least twice as likely as white women to be living in poverty.
+ Only a quarter of all adult women (age 18 and older) with incomes below the poverty line are single mothers.
+ Women are paid less than men, even when they have the same qualifications and work the same hours. And women face a greater risk of poverty.

It can be a terrible thing to be pushed to the margins, to be ostracized, to be disenfranchised, to be without advocacy, to have no one to speak up for you or to lift a voice in your behalf. It can be a terrible thing to be one of those that Dr. Samuel Proctor described as being born behind the scratch line, meaning that just as some of us inherited benefits that we do not deserve, some have inherited deficits that they do not deserve. It can be a terrible thing to fall through the cracks.

There are many who know what it feels like to fall through the cracks, to be rendered voiceless or invisible because of poverty, because of gender, because of race, because of economic status, because of age and ethnicity. And if we have been fortunate to escape these realities, we know of someone who has fallen through the cracks. They're in every family, in every church, and on every job.

The sister in this text would be in the population who had fallen through the cracks. She would have needed affordable health care but possibly wouldn't qualify because she was living below the poverty line, for the text says that she had spent all of her living. She has no name and no identity like many women in scripture. We know nothing about her or her family tree. Mark provides no information about her marital, economic, or social status. We don't know her name, but she is described by her symptoms. She is a woman with a flow of blood and she has suffered with this "issue" for 12 years. The problem was not that she had a flow of blood, for the flow of blood is normal for women, but this woman's problem had lasted too long and was continual.

And there is nothing like having an issue, a sickness, a problem, a dilemma, a situation, or suffering that lasts too long or won't seem to go away. Someone has faced a situation where it seemed that the more things change the more they remain the same. Someone has had a problem that lasted too long, a relationship that lasted too long, an assignment that lasted too long, and a hardship that lasted too long. There are many with the testimony that the more things change, the more they remain the same. This woman had a problem that lasted too long. She had been suffering for 12 years.

Twelve years is a long time. It's a long time to be broke, unemployed, caught up in a toxic unproductive relationship, and it's a long time to be sick, or miserable. Twelve years is a long time to be stuck in the same place. And depending upon the situation and its severity, 12 months or 12 days can be a long time. I have lived through and lived with some situations that have tested my patience, my faith, and my resilience because long-term issues have a way of wearing on us. Long-term suffering can take its toll on us. It can leave us feeling powerless, hopeless, and void of strength, joy, and peace. It can leave us too weak to negotiate the normal responsibilities of life and living. No doubt this woman's suffering had taken its toll.

We cannot be certain what caused this woman's internal hemorrhaging, but we can be certain that she was a very sick woman. Not only had she suffered, but she lived with the stigma of her disease. Stigma is a powerful and discrediting social label that affects the way individuals view themselves and the way they are viewed by others. Stigma reduces a person from wholeness to a statistic, to a discounted second-class status. Stigma results in exclusion and isolation as a result of one's status.

This woman lived with the stigma of her disease because she had an issue of blood that had lasted too long. One should not confuse her problem with the regular menstrual cycle, which is a normal part of life. Her perpetual bleeding was abnormal and her case was serious.

Continuous bleeding carried major implications for her in those days. Leviticus 15:19-30 contains social and sanitary laws for menstruating women. According to the law, she was considered ceremonially or ritually unclean. Her impurity was transmissible to others until her problem could be rectified. Anyone touching her clothes, chair, bed, and the like became ceremonially unclean, and anyone she touched became unclean and would be required to bathe and launder their clothing.

The stigma of ritual uncleanness resulted in social contamination. Her condition left her on the fringes of society and excluded her from normal social contact and religious or cultic activity. She needed to be quarantined. She was excluded from temple worship while unclean and could not mingle with crowds in the streets or in the market. In a society where honor was a pivotal value, her appearance in public without companions may have indicated "shame status." Because of the nature of her illness, she had been excluded from community and active participation in society for twelve years. She is outside the religious community and the honorable human community.

She lives with a diminished sense of self-worth. She has no one to speak up for her, no father like Jairus to appeal to Jesus in her behalf. She is a nobody. No doubt she has probably been the recipient of all kinds of distorted messages about her value, worth, and personhood. And to make matters even worse, she has spent all of her living and instead of getting better she is getting worse. It's quite possible that she would have been counted among the uninsured who would fall between the cracks. Her sickness probably kept her from working. With no job, she has no income and with no income, she can't pay her bills. She has been drained of her resources and there is no affordable health care.

This woman heard about Jesus of Nazareth, who was administering free health care. Jesus, the Palestinian Jew from the hood. Jesus, who was one of the disinherited. Jesus, who went about doing good. Perhaps she heard about how Jesus cast an evil spirit out of a man in the synagogue. Perhaps she heard how he healed Peter's mother-in-law of an excruciating fever, and how he healed many sick and demon-possessed people. She must have heard about how Jesus healed a man with leprosy and a paralyzed man, and how he healed a man with a withered hand. She must have heard about how Jesus calmed a raging storm and exorcised a legion of demons out of a man who had been living among the tombs. This suffering, sick, stigmatized woman must have heard about what Jesus did for others, and on the basis of his reputation she decided to seek his help.

I believe that on the basis of the reports she had heard concerning Jesus, she was convinced that if he could heal leprosy and fevers, cast out devils, and calm the tempest, then surely he could make her whole. That's probably how she ended up in the crowd on that day. Her very life depended upon her getting to Jesus.

Blood is fundamental to the function of every cell of every component in our bodies. Cells need food to survive, grow, repair, fulfill their specific functions, and reproduce. Cellular food is transported in blood to provide energy for all the cells' needs. We are multicellular organisms, having separate specialized organs with highly sophisticated functions. Transport and communication between these structures is essential. For life is in the blood; so says Leviticus 17:11. We must have enough blood flowing around our body or else our bodily functions deteriorate and we die.

This woman had been bleeding 12 years!!! Her very life depended on getting to Jesus!!!

But there is a slight problem: she is in the crowd with Jesus, but she is not on his itinerary.

Jesus is on his way to Jairus's house, the ruler of the Synagogue. Jairus is desperate, too, for Jesus to heal his 12-year-old daughter who is also at the point of death.

On the surface, Jairus seems to have the advantage. He is male, ritually pure, and holds a religious office. The woman, on the other hand, is unnamed, female, impure, impoverished, and destitute. But notice that despite everything that is working against her—stigma, status, and sickness, she refuses to resign herself to live like this forever. Despite her stigma, her status, and her sickness, she refused to accept her issue as permanent.

And there are people who have accepted the report that their "issue" is permanent. That this is as good as it gets, that their best days are behind them, and that the odds are stacked against them. And the enemy of our souls tries to use what looks like hopeless situations to exploit our faith and convince us that it is our destiny to live a hopeless existence and that we may as well resign ourselves to an unprofitable destiny.

And sometimes it can be very tempting to "resign"—to resign from life, resign from the faith, resign from believing that we still have hope and a future. Sometimes life is like a game of Words with Friends or a bad hand of spades, when it seems that there is no way we can win with the hand we have before us. But thank God that this woman resolves—she decides firmly—on a course of action. She has a firm determination to do something—she makes up her mind to do whatever it takes.

Rutgers paralyzed football player Eric LeGrand resolved that he would graduate from college despite his severe spinal cord injury. He told the crowd at his commencement, "Don't ever let someone tell you that you can't do something." Gabby Douglas resolved that she would be an Olympic champion. Nehemiah resolved that he would rebuild Jerusalem's walls despite the opposition of Sanballat and Tobiah. David resolved that he would slay Goliath in spite of his size. And the woman with the issue of blood refused to resign herself to an unprofitable destiny. She resolved, I can't live the rest of my life like this and whatever it takes I'm going to reach out and touch Jesus. She believed that Jesus' touch had power. She takes a risk of faith and the risk paid off.

And may I suggest that every now and then, we have to talk to ourselves like that woman and refuse to accept our issue as permanent. Every now and then we have to be desperate enough to break the rules and declare, "Whatever it takes, I'm going to touch Jesus."

This woman was desperate enough to break the rules, because she was determined to touch Jesus. And so even though she didn't have an appointment, even though she was just a face in the thronging crowd, even though Jesus was headed to heal Jairus's 12-year-old daughter, Mark says that when she heard of Jesus, she came up behind him and said, "If I can but touch the hem of his garment, I shall be made whole."

May I suggest that some of us, if not all of us, have been behind in a lot of things, behind in our dreams, in our resolutions, behind in our finances, behind in our goals, behind in our spiritual growth, but there comes a time when we have to do what that woman with the flow of blood did and take a risk of faith.

Perhaps you are in some stressful situations and you were just about to resign—resign from life, resign from the faith, resign from believing that you still have hope and a future. But in spite of what the situation is, you must resolve to do what the woman with the issue of blood did. You must take the risk. You must reach out and touch Jesus. If Jesus could heal that woman with the issue of blood, if Jesus could give sight to the blind, if Jesus could unstop deaf ears, if Jesus could raise Lazarus from the dead, if Jesus could feed a multitude with two fish and five loaves of bread, then surely, surely Jesus can turn your situation around.

I might be coming up from behind, but I'm gonna go for it, for my healing, for my deliverance, for my breakthrough. Today is my day to take my life back, because the same Jesus who healed that woman is the same Jesus who can turn my situation around, heal my body, deliver my children, save my marriage, and restore my finances.

And I refuse to die like this. I can't die sick, I can't die broke, I can't die frustrated, I can't die depressed. "NOW" faith is the substance of things hoped for, the evidence of things not seen! I'm going to reach out and touch the hem of his garment! I'm going to take the risk of faith!

CHAPTER 5

I CAN PRODUCE

> Meanwhile, the people were waiting for Zechariah and won-
> dering why he stayed so long in the temple. When he came out,
> he could not speak to them. They realized he had seen a vision
> in the temple, for he kept making signs to them but remained
> unable to speak. When his time of service was completed, he
> returned home. After this his wife Elizabeth became pregnant
> and for five months remained in seclusion. "The Lord has done
> this for me," she said. "In these days he has shown his favor and
> taken away my disgrace among the people."
> —LUKE 1:21-25, NIV

I HAVE A PASTOR FRIEND, REV. KEITH NORMAN (PASTOR OF
First Baptist Broad Church in Memphis), who loves watch-
ing cartoons. When Charles Schulz, the writer of the *Peanuts*
comic strip, died in 2004, Pastor Keith made an interesting observation about the characters in *Peanuts*. He said, "You know,
I really liked reading the Peanuts comic strip but I was a little
disappointed with Charlie Schultz when he died because it
seemed that everybody in the comic strip seemed to change
or get a second chance except a character by the name of Pig-
Pen. Pig Pen was the character in the Peanuts comic strip who
was always surrounded by a cloud of dust. Everywhere Pig Pen
went, he was followed by dirt and dust. Charlie Brown never
got a chance to kick the football, but at least he figured out
that he couldn't kick the ball. Lucy, who seemed to always be

cranky and mean, finally did act nice. Linus, who always carried around the blanket, finally reached an age of maturity and grew up. Schroeder, who introduced us to Bach and Beethoven, finally said something. Snoopy stopped being mischievous long enough to help Woodstock. Franklin, the only Black child in the *Peanuts* comic strip, finally got some lines. But Pig Pen's story never changed. When Pig Pen was introduced in 1954, in a comic strip scene with a blonde-headed girl named Sally and Peppermint Patty, Sally walks over to Pig Pen and inquires about his name. Pig Pen responded by saying, 'They call me Pig Pen.' And almost fifty years later, at Charlie Schulz's death, Pig Pen's story never gets rewritten."[1]

From the time that Pig Pen is introduced in 1954 until Schulz's death in 2004, *the dominating story* in Pig Pen's life is one in which he walked around surrounded by a cloud of dust.

In his book *Recalling Our Own Stories: Spiritual Renewal for Religious Caregivers*, Dr. Edward Wimberly states that "in the process of spiritual renewal, an exploration of the concept of mythology is immensely helpful. Mythology refers to the beliefs and the convictions that people have about themselves, their relationships with others, their roles in life and their ministry. It refers to the way beliefs and convictions are constructed and how these constructions shape our lives and our behavior."[2]

Wimberly suggests that we find in our lives a dominant story or myth out of which we come, while the other stories or myths in our lives become sub-myths or secondary myths. The dominant myth, which Wimberly also refers to as the project of existence (which is the over-arching framework in an individual's life that gives meaning and shape to everything that goes on—or the vocational window or umbrella through which we look at all of what we do, the roadmap for fulfilling our call) gives meaning and shape to our lives.[3] For some, the dominant story might be that they were embattled heroes working against great odds, like Rosa Parks, who wouldn't give up her seat on her bus; Sojourner Truth, who worked tirelessly for the abolition of slavery; Ida B. Wells-Barnett, who spoke out against lynching; Shirley Chisholm, who coined the phrase that she was unbought and unbossed and believed that even if she couldn't win the presidency, some black girl needed to see that in America a black woman could run for president; and Fannie Lou Hamer, who would not be satisfied until Blacks had the right to vote. This dominant story originates with God, who sets this dominant story in motion in our lives, and this dominant story is being renewed by God day by day to bring renewal to our lives.

But while there is a dominant story, Wimberly proposes that the dominant story is often eclipsed by "the lesser stories or sub-myths that often take center stage in our lives."[4] When this happens, we suffer loss of meaning and direction. The sub-myths or lesser myths often emerge from our experience as human beings. They emerge from social, cultural, political, and yes, even religious realities. They function best when they are in line with our project of existence or our call, when they are being renewed daily by the ongoing call of our lives. However, sometimes the sub-myths of our lives are so challenging and powerful that they block the influence of the ongoing call.

Pig Pen's lesser story was that he was always surrounded by a cloud of dust. Much like Pig Pen, we have inherited lesser stories and sub-myths that take center stage in our lives so that even now lesser stories are still taking center stage in the lives of women who have been gifted and graced for ministry. Despite all of the strides made for women, there are still lesser stories that attempt to eclipse the dominant story of our existence and block the ongoing call of God in our lives.

Sexism continues to undermine and destroy a vision of gender justice and gender equality because it is built upon a faulty notion that induces an attitude of inferiority upon the basis of gender with no regard for a woman's unique gifts, graces, abilities, and skills. Even in these times, there is still a soft bigotry of low expectations because of cultural biases that equate brain power with gender and assumes that women are incompetent because of our gender and that we cannot do a job as well as a man.

In the 21st century, we still suffer from bibliolatry that idolizes texts that are used to keep women and the marginalized oppressed with passages such as 1 Corinthians 14:34: "Let your women keep silence in the churches: for it is not permitted unto them to speak; but they are commanded to be under obedience as also saith the law."[5]

Some women are still laboring within and under patriarchal structures that affirm women's gifts and teaching, serving as superintendents of Sunday schools, raising money for pastor's appreciations, serving, cooking, and cleaning, but that tell us that we cannot preach. Many women preachers are still being labeled by the misogynists and sexist women as lesbians, transvestites, and gay. In the 21st century, there are still people who even tell members of the church where I serve that they are out of the will of God and that they are going to hell because their pastor is a woman.

These are just some of the lesser stories, or sub-myths, that compete for center stage in our lives. For some of us these lesser stories have resulted in a loss of meaning and direction, a second-guessing of God's intentions/plans for our lives, and they get in the way of our fulfilling the ongoing call.

The sister in the text was familiar with the challenge of living with lesser stories, sub-myths, and lies because the lesser story of her life was that she was old and childless or barren. Barrenness (the inability to conceive children, particularly sons) in scripture is an image of lifelessness, where God's redemptive blessing is absent. Not only was barrenness an image of lifelessness, but it was considered a curse, and in some cases it was grounds for divorce.

In the Bible fruitful land and fertile women are images of the blessedness of life as God had originally intended it. The opposite—unproductive, sterile, and infertile—was characterized in biblical images as the consequences of sin. The image of the barren wife is one of the Bible's strongest images of desolation and rejection. Elizabeth is in the company of women like Sarah, the wife of Abraham; Rebekah, the wife of Isaac; Rachel, the wife of Jacob; Manoah's wife, Samson's mother; and Hannah, one of Eli's wives. These are striking examples of the priority placed upon images of fertility in scripture.

Elizabeth's barrenness was further complicated by the fact that she lived in an unapologetically patriarchal culture, where the individual value of a woman was shaped by a social structure that sustained and perpetuated male dominance over females. This social construct also defined the relationship between women and men as one of subordination and domination. Women were subordinate to men in power and were economically dependent upon them for survival. The world in which Elizabeth lived was embedded with rules that did not include women. In a word, women in ancient culture were viewed as little more than property. A woman's redemption was in childbearing.

Now it is important to note that both Elizabeth and Zachariah were of priestly descent. Zechariah was from the priestly order of Abijah, and Elizabeth was from the priestly line of Aaron.[6] We know who Aaron was. He was the brother of Moses and Miriam, initially assigned to be Moses' mouthpiece, and who later became the ancestor of the priestly tribe of Aaron, and the paradigm for later priests.

Both Elizabeth and Zechariah were from a priestly order *and* from a righteous remnant waiting for the coming of the Messiah, careful to do all that the Lord commanded. But Elizabeth's dominant story of *priestly heritage* was overshadowed by her lesser story of barrenness. Although the story that should have given meaning and shape to her life was that she was a righteous woman, a woman from a priestly lineage, the lesser story or sub-myth or the lie that took center stage in her life was that she was barren—an image of isolation and desolation, reproach, shame, and disgrace. It appeared that Elizabeth's story would end without ever changing.

Ah, but after being childless, hopeless, and humiliated for many years because of the perceived "curse" that was upon their lives, and at a time when they were too old to expect any change in their situation, an angel appeared to Zechariah while he was carrying out his priestly duties to inform Zechariah that God was about to re-edit, or re-author, their lesser story to bring it in line with their ongoing call.

Elizabeth, who was barren, would bear a son. They would name him John and he would be the forerunner of Jesus Christ. "He will be great in the sight of the Lord . . . filled with the Holy Spirit even before he is born. He will bring back many of the people of Israel to the Lord their God. And he will go on before the Lord, in the spirit and power of Elijah, to turn the hearts of the parents to their children and the disobedient to the wisdom of the righteous—to make ready a people prepared for the Lord."[7]

When Zechariah heard the news, he expressed doubt regarding the possibility, but God brought it to pass. Ah, but Elizabeth knew what time it was. The Bible says that when she conceived, she said, "The Lord has done this for me. In these days he has shown his favor and taken away my disgrace among the people."[8]

In a word, Elizabeth is saying that God has moved me from shame to self-worth. The lesser story or sub-myth of my life has been brought back in line with the ongoing call for my life. For a woman whose story appeared as though it would end as an image of desolation, God took the liberty of rewriting her story. Barrenness was not her destiny because of the grace of God that was unfolding in her life. In so many words, Elizabeth is saying, "I can produce. I know what the culture says—that I am too old and I am barren, but through the grace of God at work in my life, I can produce."

Produce by definition means: 1. To bring forth (a product), to bear, give, yield. 2. To form by artistic effort: compose, create, and write. 3. To bring (a product or idea, for example) into being: to develop, generate. To create by forming, combining, or altering materials: assemble, build, construct, fabricate, fashion, forge, frame, make, manufacture, mold, put together, shape. To cause to come into existence: beget, breed, create, engender, father, hatch, make, originate, parent, procreate, sire, spawn, to give birth (or rise) to.

In my homilectical imagination, I can hear Elizabeth saying, "I can produce! I am capable of giving birth to something because of the grace of God that is work within me. I can give birth to something! Oh yes, yes, yes, I can produce!"

Yes, there are lesser stories, there are sub-myths, there are lies that seek to take center-stage: we are women, we are Black, we are single, we are divorced, we have been abused, we have been raped, we have been molested, we have been rejected—but we can produce! We are disabled, we are visually challenged, we are childless, we are husbandless—but we can produce! We have been told you can't, you ain't supposed to, you won't, and you didn't ask us if you could, but we can produce!

And so the question is, Whose report will you believe? We shall believe the report of the Lord. His report says, I am made in his image, created in his likeness, endowed with position and destiny that is just a little lower than the angels. His report says, We have this treasure in earthen jars that the excellency of the power may be of God and not of us. I can produce! And we can produce more than babies! We can produce books, electronic journals, music, songs, women's organizations, sermons, ideas, opinions, artistic compositions, ministries for wounded women, ministries for the hurting, and ministries for the overlooked, the left-out, and the looked-over.

Elizabeth's story is our proof that barrenness does not have to have the last word for our lives, for nothing is impossible with God. We can produce! I can produce!

NOTES

1. Rev. Keith Norman, Pastor of First Baptist Broad Church, Memphis, Tennessee, CMBC Lenten Noon Day Worship.

2. Edward P. Wimberly, *Recalling Our Own Stories: Spiritual Renewal for Religious Caregivers* (San Francisco, CA: Jossey-Bass, 1997).

3. Ibid.

4. Ibid.

5. 1 Corinthians 14:34, KJV.

6. Luke 1:5.

7. Luke 1:15-17, NIV.

8. Luke 1:25, NIV.

CHAPTER 6

THE AUDACITY
OF FAITH

Leaving that place, Jesus withdrew to the region of Tyre and
Sidon. A Canaanite woman from that vicinity came to him, crying out, "Lord, Son of David, have mercy on me! My daughter is
demon-possessed and suffering terribly."

Jesus did not answer a word. So his disciples came to him and
urged him, "Send her away, for she keeps crying out after us." He
answered, "I was sent only to the lost sheep of Israel." The woman
came and knelt before him. "Lord, help me!" she said. He replied,
"It is not right to take the children's bread and toss it to the dogs."
"Yes it is, Lord," she said. "Even the dogs eat the crumbs that fall
from their master's table."

—MATTHEW 15:21-27, NIV

JESUS HAS JUST COMPLETED A HECTIC MINISTRY IN THE RE-
gion of Galilee in the area of Capernaum, which was the head-
quarters for Jesus' ministry. After having interacted with the
crowds and experiencing a head-on collision with conflict with
Jewish leaders from Jerusalem, Jesus and his disciples travelled
outside the boundaries of Israel to Gentile cities in the region
of Tyre. The people who lived there were not Jews; they did not
follow the religion of Israel. They were Gentiles—outside the
covenant or outsiders.

The text offers no explanation for Jesus' decision to go into
the region, but it is quite possible that Jesus withdrew to this

area for a time of retreat and rest from the crowds. Jesus had an incredible magnetic ministry and he was always drawing crowds. His ministry was so impactful that crowds or multitudes were always following him with incessant needs. It seems that wherever Jesus went, the crowds had a way of finding him. That is no surprise because wherever Jesus went, he made an impact: blind received their sight, tempests subsided, the deaf began to hear again, and the lame started to walk again. Jesus even raised people from the dead. He restored dignity to the poor and marginalized and to women. He loosed captives from the crippling influences, he re-established wholeness and equilibrium to the lives of God's people, and he neutralized the power of sin to bring just about everyone he came in contact with to a state of uprightness. So it would come as no surprise that crowds would follow Jesus.

Religious leaders were always tracking him on their radar, looking for any infraction for no other purpose than to create controversy or discredit his ministry. So Jesus could probably use the rest. The end of his ministry is approaching, and the intensity of opposition is increasing. He can find no solitude in Galilee where the people are, but this region Tyre ought to be different, for Tyre is the region of the Phoenicians, and the Phoenicians would have no desire to interact with Jesus.

Because unlike Galilee and Capernaum, this area was much more Gentile and Greek. This is an area known for its paganism.

Tyre is a place known in the Old Testament as being wicked. It's the hometown of Jezebel, one of the famous villains of the Hebrew Scriptures. Josephus, the Jewish historian, described the people of Tyre are "as our bitterest enemies." Thus the region of Tyre and Sidon was a great place to avoid controversy, crowds, and critics.

But even here, Jesus is not to be left alone. A Canaanite woman from that region came to Jesus. It's interesting that Matthew uses the word "Canaanite" to describe her. Mark calls her

"Syrophoenician" woman but Matthew calls her a "Canaanite." Matthew uses an Old Testament word for the people who were living in the land of Canaan back when the Israelites moved in.

The Canaanites were Gentiles, pagans by culture, by language a Greek and by religion a pagan (non-Jew) outside of the covenant the Lord had made with Abraham. Yet they were in close-enough contact, close-enough proximity, to have some knowledge about the religion of Israel.

And this nameless woman apparently did. For she comes to Jesus asking for help because she has a problem. Problems and suffering have a way of driving us *to* the Lord or *away from* the Lord. One of the benefits of suffering, strange as it may seem, is that it can lead us to seek the Lord and His mercy.

It is ironic that when life is going well for us we tend to place God on the margin of our lives and tend to take God's blessings for granted. We don't really renounce God or completely abandon our faith—we just relegate God to the periphery. God is not completely out of the picture—God just doesn't occupy as dominant a place in our lives.

But when suffering comes, and we have no one else to turn to, nowhere else to go—it's amazing how quickly we gain a sharper focus and how quickly we fix our eyes on the Lord. Suffering has a way of driving us to our knees. Many a believer would be pressed to admit that their prayer life has been strengthened by suffering. In her book *The Sound of Intercession*, Dr. Claudette Copeland states that "God will mercifully construct circumstances—even those that seem to be demonically inspired to do one thing—to cause us to bend our knees and chase after God, for some of us have found out that God will hear us in our day of trouble."[1]

That's what this woman is doing when she comes to Jesus. It's her "day of trouble," and she's calling on God for help. And so, because it is her day of trouble, she comes to Jesus, crying out, "Lord, Son of David. Have mercy on me." She uses the Messianic term "Son of David," for the anointed the one God promised would be the Son of David, a physical descendant of the great King David, and the greatest one of all, even greater than David himself.

The Lord had promised David that one of his sons would reign on his throne forever. And this Son of David, this Messiah, this Christ, Jesus would usher in a glorious reign of blessing for Israel and for all the other nations, too. When the Messiah comes, his blessing would extend to the Gentiles as well as to Israel. The nations would come running to Israel in those days, to receive the Lord's blessing—just as this Canaanite woman is doing now, in coming to Jesus because it is her day of trouble.

So even though she is an outsider, this woman could have possibly known the prophecies about the coming Messiah, the Son of David. She must have recognized Jesus as the fulfillment of those prophecies.

It is almost as if she knows about the Messianic secret. Frequently in the Gospels, especially in Mark, Jesus is portrayed as trying to maintain an element of secrecy about himself and his work. Today, this feature is referred to as the "messianic secret."[2] Throughout the Gospel of Mark, Jesus made every attempt to conceal His true identity as the Christ.[3] Matthew understood the messianic secret as the fulfillment of prophecy.[4] Throughout the gospel of Mark, Jesus suppressed their confession. He prohibited public profession by those who experienced miraculous healing (Mark 1:43-44; 5:43; 7:36). The parables of Jesus were offered in order to keep "outsiders" from learning the secret (Mark 4:11-12). Even the disciples, once they understood the "secret of the kingdom of God" (Mark 4:11), were sworn to silence.[5]

But it seems that even though this woman is an outsider and a Gentile, it appears that she has "inside information" about Jesus. It seems that she has heard some things about Jesus that the others don't know or care about. Perhaps she heard what Jesus was doing, his healings, his miracles, his acts of mercy. She must have known or heard enough about Jesus that it emboldened her to come forward with her request. There was something that drew her to Jesus as the answer to her problems.

She said, "Have mercy on me."[6] Notice that she doesn't cry for justice or equality. She isn't attempting to lay claim to any benefit or perks. She is asking for something that she knows by virtue of her race and religion that she is not entitled to.

"Lord, have mercy." Several times in the Gospels we hear people crying out to Jesus with these words. Blind men asking for their sight. A father seeking help for his demonized son. And this woman is a mother seeking similar help for her daughter, who was suffering terribly.

This woman came to Jesus because she needed something that society had not been able to provide. She was looking for something that her dead religion had been powerless to give her. She needed a solution that she had not been able to provide by her own self-efforts. She was desperate and she saw Jesus as her only hope! And she really takes a chance because she has several obstacles working against her.

First of all, she is from the wrong place. She is from the region of Tyre and Sidon. Tyre and Sidon were technically outside the boundaries of Israel. It had been promised originally to Israel, but they had never really conquered Tyre and Sidon. Tyre and Sidon was Gentile country.

Secondly, she comes from the wrong people. She was a Canaanite. Not only does she live in the wrong place, but she is a Gentile, specifically a Canaanite.

Canaanites were enemies of God's people. They belonged to different cultures, to different religions, and they had different histories. She's an outsider. She's not one of the religiously privileged people, the people Jesus came to talk to. She is the descendent of an ancient, proud, and accomplished people, a nation of merchants and seafarers who at one time had dominated the entire Mediterranean and had vied with Rome for the control of the known world. She is a descendant from what was believed to be a cursed people and a doomed race. She was from a region known for vile religious practices.

But not only is she a Gentile, from Gentile territory, but by most estimations, she is not really considered a person. She is a woman, which by most estimations in those days she was not a person. In the first century, women were marginalized and often lived with the reality of gender bias.

This woman from the wrong place and the wrong people was a mother with a sick child who wanted relief for her daughter. Even if you don't have children of your own, you can imagine what she must have been going through. She had carried this baby in her womb for nine months. She's been through the travail of labor and delivery. She has experienced the pain of childbirth. She has washed, fed, and clothed her daughter. She watched her grow, heard her first word, and rejoiced when she took her first step.

Maybe her daughter had been sick before with a cold or a fever, or even the flu, but nothing like this. Her daughter is being tormented by a demon. And we know that the devil and his demons don't play fair. He comes to steal, kill, and destroy. No doubt her daughter is screaming and shouting, out of control, strange voices coming out of her mouth. Her behavior is far from normal. She probably can't sleep, eat, or play because she is grievously tormented by the devil.

And I can imagine that by the time Jesus makes it to her region that it is her desperation that makes her bold. She could have easily given up in frustration, but she didn't. In her desperation, she makes her way to Jesus. She interrupts his sabbatical to ask for some help, because delivering helpless people is His specialty.

Good news travels fast doesn't it? Good news travels far and wide. Jesus is in her vicinity. Verse 22 tells us that she was so desperate that she cried out for mercy. When you're sick you need a doctor. When you have a legal problem you need a lawyer. When you're having family problems you go to a counselor. When you're having trouble in school you find a personal tutor. When you're having problems with your pipes you need a plumber. But if your problem is demon-possession, you need a demon-chaser, a yoke -breaker, a hell-raiser. You need Jesus.

And because she needed Jesus, despite all that she had working against her she had *audacity*. Audacity: some would call it holy chutzpah—boldness, presumptuousness—a certain audacity.

She had boldness or daring or the willingness to challenge assumptions or conventions or tackle something difficult or dangerous. She had audacity.

Audacity is what Barack Obama had when he decided to run for President. Audacity is what Martin King and those brave men and women had when they marched on the Edmund Pettus bridge in Selma, Alabama, despite death threats and constant scrutiny by J. Edgar Hoover and demands to call the march off from the White House. Audacity is what the woman with the issue of blood had to think that she could touch the hem of Jesus' garment and be made whole. Audacity is what Joshua had when he told the sun to stand still. Audacity is what Daniel had when he kept on praying even though an edict had been signed that anybody found praying would be thrown into a lions' den. Audacity is what Shadrach, Meshach, and Abednego had when they refused to bow to Nebuchadnezzar's golden image.

Audacity is what made Gabby Douglas believe she could win the Olympics. Audacity is what made King stand up to President Lyndon Baines Johnson and demand that the law be changed so that African Americans who were already free could register to vote without opposition. Audacity is what makes people in third world or developing countries believe that they can change the world with limited resources—and they do it. Audacity is what every preacher has every time she or he mounts the pulpit to challenge believers to pursue God's best for their lives.

This woman had what I call the audacity of faith because even though she was a Gentile, she had the spiritual courage to ask Jesus for the impossible even when the odds were stacked against her.

She cries out, "Have mercy on me, O Lord, Son of David. For my daughter is possessed by a demon that torments her severely." Just judging from her request, she seems to know even though she is a Gentile that Jesus is the answer to her problem. But she had the audacity to ask Jesus for the help she needed despite the barriers. And the text says that her faith was rewarded.

Who among us doesn't know the frustration of feeling that the odds are stacked against you? Perhaps you don't have a sick child or a demon-possessed child, but you are dealing with a child who is out of control. Perhaps you are at your wits end over some situation that seems to be in reverse or that you are stuck on park. Or maybe you have exhausted every means at your disposal and do not know where to turn for help. Maybe what you need is salvation. Or maybe what you need is deliverance, salvation, restoration, or forgiveness.

I dare you to have the audacity to ask the Savior to help you. Audacious faith is indispensable to lifting limits. This woman is a classic example that despite limiting conditions, audacious faith will propel us to ask God *for* the impossible. And here is the reason we can ask God for the impossible: because God is a God *of* the impossible.

And because this Canaanite woman had the audacity to ask for the impossible, Jesus did what seemed impossible. Jesus eventually gave her what she asked her. Because of her audacious faith, her daughter was healed at that moment. Hallelujah, Let the name of the Lord be praised!

Notes

1. Claudette A. Copeland, *The Sound of Intercession* (Windcrest: Red Nail Press, 2014).

2. C. M. Tuckett, "Messianic Secret," in D. N. Freedman (ed.), *The Anchor Yale Bible Dictionary, Vol. 4* (New York: Doubleday, 1992), 797.

3. R. Reeves, "Messianic Secret," in C. Brand, C. Draper, A. England, S. Bond, E. R. Clendenen, & T. C. Butler (eds.), *Holman Illustrated Bible Dictionary* (Nashville, TN: Holman Bible Publishers, 2003), 1116.

4. Ibid.

5. Ibid.

6. Matthew 15:22.

CHAPTER 7

FOR SUCH A TIME
AS THIS

When Mordecai learned of all that had been done, he tore his clothes, put on sackcloth and ashes, and went out into the city, wailing loudly and bitterly. But he went only as far as the king's gate, because no one clothed in sackcloth was allowed to enter it. In every province to which the edict and order of the king came, there was great mourning among the Jews, with fasting, weeping and wailing. Many lay in sackcloth and ashes.

When Esther's eunuchs and female attendants came and told her about Mordecai, she was in great distress. She sent clothes for him to put on instead of his sackcloth, but he would not accept them. Then Esther summoned Hathak, one of the king's eunuchs assigned to attend her, and ordered him to find out what was troubling Mordecai and why.

So Hathak went out to Mordecai in the open square of the city in front of the king's gate. Mordecai told him everything that had happened to him, including the exact amount of money Haman had promised to pay into the royal treasury for the destruction of the Jews. He also gave him a copy of the text of the edict for their annihilation, which had been published in Susa, to show to Esther and explain it to her, and he told him to instruct her to go into the king's presence to beg for mercy and plead with him for her people. Hathak went back and reported to Esther what Mordecai had said. Then she instructed him to say to Mordecai, "All the king's officials and the people of the royal provinces know that for any man or woman who approaches the king in the inner court without being summoned the king has but one law: that they be put to death unless the king extends the gold scepter to them and spares their lives. But thirty days have passed since I was called to go to the king."

When Esther's words were reported to Mordecai, he sent back this answer: "Do not think that because you are in the king's house you alone of all the Jews will escape. For if you remain silent at this time, relief and deliverance for the Jews will arise from another place, but you and your father's family will perish. And who knows but that you have come to your royal position for such a time as this?"

—Esther 4:1-14, NIV

February 11, 2011 was a defining moment in Egypt's history when Hosni Mubarak resigned as president and handed control to the military after 29 years in power, bowing to an historic 18-day wave of pro-democracy demonstrations by hundreds of thousands. Images of several hundred thousand protesters in Cairo were seen cheering and waving. Egyptian flags were seen around the world. Fireworks, car horns, and celebratory shots in the air were heard around the city of 18 million in joy after the Egyptian Vice President made the announcement on national TV.

Defining moments are important because as the historic transfer of power in Egypt indicates, defining moments have the power to change our lives, and they create the critical mass from which new habits are born. Priorities change and paradigms shift because a dramatic pause in our life forces us to examine what is really important or to gain clarity about something that has previously eluded us.

Defining moments occur when one consciously chooses to do something or stop doing something or when something becomes as obvious as the nose on our face. Defining moments can be specific and personal, such as the dissolution of a marriage, the death of a spouse, walking off a dead-end job, accepting the call to preach, stepping out to open a business, taking the first plane ride, a first date, or even a first kiss.

Defining moments can also be societal and communal. Many of us have witnessed many defining moments in history: the assassination of President John F. Kennedy, Robert F. Kennedy, Malcolm X, and Martin Luther King Jr.; the fall of Communism; the Great Depression; the Great Recession of the 21st century; the dismantling of Apartheid; the fall of the twin towers; and the election of the first African American President.

It was a communal defining moment in 1955 when the communal outrage over Rosa Parks's arrest unified the African American community to stage a large-scale boycott against Montgomery City bus lines.

It was a communal defining moment in the life of the church of my childhood when on March 4, 1995, the Christ Missionary Baptist Church of Memphis, Tennessee, decided to take a courageous step and decided to elect one of its "daughters," the Rev. Dr. Gina M. Stewart, to lead their congregation.

And some of you have experienced your own personal defining moments: Perhaps it was the day you walked away from an abusive and toxic relationship, the day you decided to stop neglecting yourself while taking care of everybody else, the day you decided to go to school or to drop out of school, the day you decided to stop enabling a child, a spouse, a lover or a loved one, or a friend.

Defining moment are "crisis" points (or pivot points) that may have a variety of outcomes. Whenever we experience defining moments we think differently, feel differently, and act differently. Our view of life is different and our perceptions change, and in many instances, we change and we are never the same.

In Scripture, we find a number of defining moments. Isaiah experienced a defining moment when he saw the Lord high and lifted up in the temple in the same year that King Uzziah died.[1] Jacob experienced a defining moment after wrestling with an angel all night.[2] Abraham experienced a defining moment on

Mount Moriah when he had to decide to trust God for a sacrifice or offer up his son Isaac.[3] Mary experienced a defining moment when an angel interrupted her regularly scheduled program to bring her a special bulletin that her life would be radically altered by an unexpected pregnancy.[4]

And in the text, Esther, Queen of Persia, was faced with her own defining moment. Our text supports this notion as we are reminded of the words spoken by her cousin Mordecai: "For if you remain silent at this time, relief and deliverance will arise for the Jews from another place, but you and your father's house will perish. And who knows but that you have come to your royal position for such a time as this?"

Up until this point, Esther's story reads like a Cinderella story. After 70 years of exile, God's people were free to leave the land of their captors and return to Jerusalem.

Thousands of Jews returned with Governor Zerubbabel's blessing to aid Ezra and Nehemiah in rebuilding the walls and the faith of the city. For whatever reason, like the majority of Jews in Persia and Babylon, Mordecai and Esther chose not to return to Jerusalem but remained in Persia.

The book of Esther begins with a drunken king summoning his wife, Vashti, to dress in her royal attire and parade her beauty before his friends. Queen Vashti refused to leave the Queen's chamber where she was entertaining her guests to appear before King Ahasuerus and become a part of the debauchery. She refused to be treated as an object for the king's pleasure. That day Vashti took a moral stand against sexism. She drew a line in the sand, rejecting her society's view of women as hood ornaments to be collected by men and shown off for status. She wanted to be treated as a person, not an object.

Needless to say her behavior stunned the king and his advisors. Vashti had undermined the status quo: females had to be subservient to males; the entire culture depended on the inequality of the sexes. The most influential men of the kingdom wasted no time in making Vashti's refusal their priority.

The king was advised that her behavior "insulted every man in the empire. His advisors feared that other women if not every woman would begin to look down on her husband as soon as she heard what the queen has done . . . Wives everywhere would have no respect for their husbands."[5] Drastic measures were required.

Vashti's removal as the queen provided the impetus for Esther's entry. The king searched for a replacement, and Esther (Hadassah—her Jewish name), raised by her cousin Mordecai, was chosen to be the new queen.

If this story were a fairy tale, we would be tempted to say that all is well and they lived happily ever after, but for Esther life was not exactly a fairy tale. The king promoted a "little man" to big position; Haman became the prime minister of the empire, second to the king. But Haman was a little man in a big place, and it can be dangerous to put "little people" in big places. "Little" is not referring to physical size or stature, but "little" in terms of their own estimation of self-worth, little in terms of struggles with insecurity, little in terms of being threatened by others.

Haman was a little man in a big place and it didn't help that all of the king's servants except Mordecai would bow when Haman entered the court. Needless to say, Mordecai's behavior was a blow to Haman's ego. Driven by megalomania and a desire for preeminence, Haman began a plot to kill not only Mordecai, but the whole race of Jews. As a result of exaggeration and political engineering, Haman received permission from the king to destroy the people whom Haman said would not obey the king and were trying to overthrow his authority.

The decree was sent to all the provinces and the Jews immediately began to mourn. Mordecai mourned in front of the king's gate in sackcloth and ashes. Esther heard of it and sent clothes to him, which he refused. When she inquired about Mordecai's behavior, she was informed of the decree and Mordecai urged her to go to the king and intercede for her people.

Esther's first response was one of fear, and truthfully speaking, who could really blame her? Anyone who values his or her life is not anxious to die. And Esther was no exception. She reasoned: "All the king's servants and the people of the king's provinces know that if any man or woman goes to the king inside the inner court without being called, there is but one law—all alike are to be put to death. Only if the king holds out the golden scepter to someone, may that person live. I myself have not been called to come in to the king for thirty days."[6] Furthermore, this king—Esther's husband—is the king who removed his first queen because of her refusal to parade in front of her drunken king and his drunken friends. This was the king whom Mordecai was asking Esther to appeal to *without an invitation*.

We should be able to understand Esther's reluctance to go in to the king if only on the basis of self-preservation. She knew that she could possibly be put to death for entering the king's presence without being summoned and she had not been summoned in thirty days. Even though Esther knew that her people were facing the threat of extermination because of one maniac, Esther basically says to Mordecai, "I can't do it!"

No doubt Esther had learned a lesson from the last queen: you come when the king calls, and you don't come at any other time. Esther had also learned from the last queen that queens are easily disposable and easily replaced.

Although Esther's response to Mordecai may seem like cowardice, it is a statement of fact. If she goes to the king unsummoned, the chances are good that she will die. Furthermore, how much influence could she possibly wield with a king who has not called for her in 30 days? Esther was in a real pinch. She held a powerful position but she felt powerless because even though she was the Queen, she was subject to the same rules as everybody else. Esther had a royal position but she was not highly valued. Technically, she felt as though she was in the same boat with everybody else with very few options. Even though Esther was in the palace, perhaps her limits of

authority were confined to the harem. Perhaps Esther never expected this assignment. She had been groomed for the harem,
not to be a heroine. As Dr. Rentia Weems once stated "Esther
was chosen because she was pretty and sexy, not because she
is wise, intelligent, or a woman of ethics but because she was
pretty."* Esther could remain silent and allow the slaughter to
commence and hide behind her robe and crown, or she could
risk saying something in a hostile environment to provide a
means of salvation for her people. But if she did so, she would
be risking her own life.

Like Esther, many of us have found ourselves in uncomfort-
able situations where the injustice, oppression, disenfranchise-
ment, and marginalization of others was at our doorstep, but
we felt powerless to act or make a difference. Before we take a
stand we frequently wonder if it will be worth it. Mordecai's
words are just as true today: "And who knows but that you have
come to your royal position for such a time as this?"[7]

Who knows? Maybe that is why you are here. Who knows?
Maybe this is why you are married to a pagan Gentile. Maybe
this is why all of these coincidences happened. In other words:
Don't hide away in the home! Don't be silent! If you stay quiet
now, you will lose your part in history, and you do have a part
to play!

Mordecai's words were just what Esther needed to rise up.
Palace or no palace, robe or no robe, queen or no queen, crown
or no crown, Esther could not stand by and be a bystander in
the ongoing oppression and victimization of her people. "If I
perish, I perish," she decided. "I am going to see the king."

When Esther finally made the tough decision to act rather
than to observe in history, she agreed despite the risk to approach the king. Esther called for a fast, and after the fast, she
devised a strategy for approaching the king, even if it cost her
life. It was a defining moment for Esther.

---

* Dr. Renita J. Weems, Plenary-Daughters of Destiny Women Conference

She would do the right thing and appeal for the life of her people. When Esther decided to approach the king, she, along with her maidens, fasted and prayed. And while they were fasting and praying, and Esther was going to the king, God was working behind the scenes. For when she went to see the king, this teenager who became queen through a series of unexpected events worked within a patriarchal power structure and utilized a clever series of moves to eventually expose the diabolical plot of Haman to her husband, who then has Haman executed and a nation was saved.

The human experience shows us that it is often easier to observe history than to participate in history. It's easier to stand on the sidelines and watch than to get in the game. It's easier and safer to follow at a distance and wait for the outcome than to take a position and trust God for the outcome. An observer of history has no particular mission. An observer of history is a spectator but not a stakeholder. Observers will come to church to receive a blessing but won't be a blessing. Observers can diagnose problems but never have a prescription for the problem. Oh, it is much easier to observe history than to participate in history.

What does Esther's defining moment have to say to a 21st-century audience? Esther reminds us that when we decide to participate in history and not just observe history, God can use us to make a difference. It's not just what we do when we gather for worship on Sunday, or for a special worship celebration or a revival, but the real litmus test is what we do, the words we speak, the life we live, and the attitudes we display each day.

Esther's story reminds us that when we understand that the life of faith is a matter of participation and not just observation, the Lord really does work in discreet and mysterious ways. And we need these reminders. We need reminders that God's ways of working in our world are not always obvious.

We need reminders that God will use the unexpected to do the unexpected. You see if we read the story closely, Esther started out in the harem. Oh yes, she did, but she landed in the palace. Furthermore, she was a Jewish girl in a Persian setting. No one would have expected Esther to land in the king's house, but the Lord moves in mysterious ways, his wonders to perform.

Sometimes God uses the small things, the little things, the things that could be easily overlooked to accomplish his purposes. Paul put it this way in 1 Corinthians 1:25-29: "For the foolishness of God is wiser than human wisdom, and the weakness of God is stronger than human strength. Brothers and sisters, think of what you were when you were called. Not many of you were wise by human standards; not many were influential; not many were of noble birth. But God chose the foolish things of the world to shame the wise; God chose the weak things of the world to shame the strong. God chose the lowly things of this world and the despised things—and the things that are not—to nullify the things that are, so that no one may boast before him."[8]

There are always those times in life when we wonder where God is. Esther reminds us that there are times when God is firmly behind the scenes, and we may not see how God has been working -because we are part of God's larger plan—until well after what is taking place now.

Just as Esther was a part of God's larger plan, we are also part of God's larger plan and are included in God's larger plan. We live in an unrighteous world, so too as in the book of Esther, where God seems to be out of the picture. But thanks be to God, God is not out of the picture. God is not dead. God is still working behind the scenes of every event, from the White House to the crack house to your neighbor's house. And God moves every event for the sake of his kingdom. And God didn't just call Esther to the kingdom for such a time as this, but God has called you for such a time as this.

God may be invisible but he is always invincible. God is present in every scene and movement of our days. And God will often make God's presence known in people like Esther, people like you and me, people like Esther who will say yes to his will.

The world desperately needs individuals like you and me to be willing to follow Esther's example and stand in the gap for God. Our culture grows more decadent and sinful every moment, and I think that much of the blame falls on those of us who hesitate to speak up and act for God's truth. History is full of accounts of single individuals who have made a difference. In fact, the people who have impacted and touched our lives the most are those who decided *to act* in history and not just observe history.

Think of the decisive military battles that have turned on the axis of one heroic person. Think of the contributions of the individual lives of artists from Michelangelo and da Vinci to Beethoven. Think of the scientists, the inventors, the explorers, and the technological experts who have literally changed the course of history. Think of the impact on the church that has been made by individuals like Mother Teresa, Corrie ten Boom, Nannie Helen Burroughs, Rev. Jarena Lee, Rev. Prathia Wynn-Hall, and Bishop Vashti McKenzie, just to name a few. Think of all the Blacks who changed the course of history: Frederick Douglass, W. E. B. Du Bois, Mary McLeod Bethune, Fannie Lou Hamer, Phillis Wheatley, Langston Hughes, Jackie Robinson, Hank Aaron, Jessie Owens, Thurgood Marshall, Barbara Jordan, Nelson Mandela, Dorothy Height, Sojourner Truth, Harriet Tubman, and Barack Obama. Think about Rahab, who delivered the spies into Israel's hands; and Deborah, who won the battle against Israel's enemies; and the Widow of Zarephath, who fed the prophet Elijah; and Vashti, who said no so that Esther could say yes; and Mary, the Mother of Jesus.

But most importantly, think about Jesus, who didn't just observe history but who participated in history. As a matter of fact, Jesus stepped up to the plate. He did not regard equality with God as something to be grasped or coveted, but he emptied himself, and became obedient even to death on the cross, and God highly exalted and gave him a name that is above every name, that every knee must bow and every tongue confess that Jesus Christ is Lord, to the glory of God the Father.[9]

He was wounded for my transgressions, bruised for my iniquities; the chastisement of my peace was upon him, and by his stripes, I am healed.[10] He was hung up for my hang-ups. He was manifest in the flesh, justified in the Spirit, seen of angels, preached unto the Gentiles, believed on in the world, received into glory. And thanks be to God that right now Jesus is seated at the right hand of God making intercession for us.

It is this same Jesus who has called us to the Kingdom for such a time as this! Esther and these heroes and sheroes are not the only ones that God has called to the Kingdom for such a time as this. God is calling us to rise up for such a time as this. Yes, God is calling us! Calling us to stand up, speak up, rise up!

Remember, it is no accident that you are where you are. God has been at work, God is at work, and God still wants to work. God has acted, maybe behind the scenes, to bring you to this place so that you can have an opportunity to use your influence for Kingdom impact . . . for such a time as this.

Notes

1. Isaiah 6:1.
2. Genesis 32:22-31.
3. Genesis 22:1-18.
4. Luke 1:26-38.
5. Esther 2:13-22.
6. Esther 4:11, NIV.
7. Esther 4:14b.
8. 1 Corinthians 1:25-29, NIV.
9. Philippians 2:5-11.
10. Isaiah 53:5.

CHAPTER 8

IF JACOB DON'T CHANGE

> When the LORD saw that Leah was not loved, he enabled her to conceive, but Rachel remained childless. Leah became pregnant and gave birth to a son. She named him Reuben, for she said, "It is because the LORD has seen my misery. Surely my husband will love me now."
>
> She conceived again, and when she gave birth to a son she said, "Because the LORD heard that I am not loved, he gave me this one too." So she named him Simeon.
>
> Again she conceived, and when she gave birth to a son she said, "Now at last my husband will become attached to me, because I have borne him three sons." So he was named Levi.
>
> She conceived again, and when she gave birth to a son she said, "This time I will praise the LORD." So she named him Judah. Then she stopped having children.
>
> —GENESIS 29:31-35, NIV

I WANT TO CAUTION YOU THAT THIS STORY IS OUR STORY, for it is not just an ancient story about two women married to the same man. It is not just a story about sibling rivalry. It is not just a story about rejection, or a story about living in the shadow of a more successful or beautiful sibling.

I submit to you that in many ways, this story is our story because Leah echoes the sentiments of many who sit in our pews and pulpits week after week, gifted but overlooked, faithful but overlooked, valuable but overlooked. For many of us, that woman's story is our story, for who among us has not felt the pain associated with rejection simply because you are not beautiful like Rachel?

We live in a world that esteems "Rachel" but has little appreciation for "Leah." We live in a world where image is everything. WE line in a world of plastic surgery, lap-bands, air-brush, Botox, lipo, and gastro. We live in a world where, as Naomi Wolf states, beauty is a currency standard. This is not to suggest that we ought to resent attractive women or women who have taken steps to address their weight issues, but I am suggesting that in a world that esteems Rachel, and typically rejects or overlooks Leah, there are many people who sit in our pews week after week who understand more of what it is like to be Leah rather than Rachel.

There are people who sit in our pews each week and who know what it is like to suffer from wounded self-esteem. For every Rachel, there is a Leah who lives in the shadow of Rachel. There's a Leah who didn't grow through the incredible transformation that comes after puberty.

It matters not how much and how many others try to encourage us, we are still bothered by our imperfections. We are too fat, too thin, too tall, too short, too dark, too light. Our noses need to be fixed, our wrinkles need to be stretched, our hair needs to be thickened . . . and the list goes on and on.

This story is not just an ancient story but a real-life story because many of us, like Leah, are among the ranks of the "emotionally fatigued." Oh, you can't look at us and tell it, but there are many of us who are emotionally fatigued by the rejection of the "Jacobs" or the persons from whom we seek affirmation, acceptance, and affection.

And Jacob doesn't necessarily have to be a husband or a lover or a significant other. Jacob could be a mother, a father, or some primary person in our life whom we have looked to for acceptance, affirmation, and affection. And some of us have spent most of our lives trying to please our "Jacobs" because we have bequeathed a place of honor to "Jacob" that is undeserved in our lives.

And so, I submit to you that there is an amazing dichotomy in this text. For it is a text of pain that births liberation. In a nutshell, it is a story about an older sister who lived in the shadow of her younger sister. It is a story about a woman who was eclipsed by her sister's beauty. It is a story about a woman who was married to a man who was not just in love with someone else, but her younger sister. It is a story about a woman who experienced firsthand the pain of rejection by the primary males in her life (her father and her husband). It is a story about what it means to be rejected and tossed aside because you are not the first choice or the obvious choice.

It is a story about how rejection impact affects self-esteem and self-worth. It is a story of what can happen to our self-esteem and self-worth when we are reminded that we are not "Rachel." Not that we don't have value, we are just not Rachel. Not that we have nothing to offer or that we are non-productive, we are just not Rachel. Not that we are not precious, we are just not Rachel.

This was the dilemma that Leah found herself in. Leah, whose name means wearied or afflicted one, was the oldest daughter of Laban and the first wife of Jacob, son of the patriarch Isaac. It has been said and implied by historians that Leah was not a pretty sight. The text tells us that she was weakeyed or tender eyed, meaning that she lacked luster, charm, and beauty or even poor vision. Her younger sister Rachel, whose name meant ewe (female sheep) was the beloved one and the beloved of Jacob.

Rachel's name is an indication of her value, for in the Hebrew tradition, the lamb was to be regarded with mercy and tenderness of heart. Rachel was the apple of Jacob's eye. In fact, so great was Jacob's love for Rachel that he committed to work seven years just to have Rachel's hand in marriage. But at the end of seven years, Rachel's father, Laban, gave Leah to Jacob as a substitute for Rachel. But Jacob was "sprung." He loved Rachel so much that he was willing to work 14 years to have her hand in marriage.

Now the text doesn't tell us whether Leah loved Jacob, but it does imply that Jacob didn't love Leah. The tragedy about Leah's relationship with Jacob was not just that Jacob loved someone else. Jacob should have been free to marry whomever he wanted to marry but Laban (his father-in-law) deceived him. The original agreement was that Jacob would work for Laban for 7 years to have Rachel's hand in marriage. But it was the custom for the oldest to marry first. And so even though Jacob honored his word and worked for 7 years, when he went into consummate his marriage with his bride, Laban had flipped the script and Leach was in the tent instead of Rachel.

The fact that Laban had to trick Jacob into marrying Leah speaks volumes about Laban's opinion of his oldest daughter and Jacob's opinion of Leah. After all, Leah never made the short list for Jacob. She wasn't even on Jacob's radar for marriage; it was Laban who orchestrated this. It was customary for the oldest daughter to be married first, but to trick someone into marrying her who had no interest in her in the first place says a lot.

Leah couldn't help the way God made her. Nevertheless, Leah lacked beauty in the narrator's eyes, in her father's eyes, and obviously in Jacob's eyes. But God gave Leah something that Rachel didn't have. The text says that when the Lord saw that Leah was unloved (King James says hated), he opened her womb. Leah could produce.

May I stop here and say that even when others ignore you and overlook you, God will put something in you that nobody else has. You may not be Rachel but you have something that Rachel doesn't have. You may not look like Rachel. You may not even be the first choice or even the obvious choice, but God has put something in your hand that nobody else has. God has equipped you to carry out a plan that nobody else can carry out. You can produce! It may not be babies, but you can produce! You have the potential to bring forth something that is life-giving and affirming and good. You can produce! There is a song in you, there's a book in you, there's a ministry in you, there's a business idea in you, there's composition in you, there's an idea in you, there's a vision in you, there's a dream in you, there is something in that only you with the power of God on your side can produce!

Now the fact that God opened Leah's womb is significant because in a culture that was unapologetically patriarchal, where the individual value of a woman was shaped by a social structure that sustained and perpetuated male dominance over females, a woman's redemption was in childbearing. In a culture where the relationship between women and men was one of subjugation, subordination, and domination, and women were subordinate to men in power and economically dependent upon them for survival, a woman's worth could be recovered if she could produce. Leah could produce, and not just babies, but sons.

In the ancient way of thinking, the life of the father continued through the son. A father could die feeling that his life on earth had fulfilled its purpose when there was a son to perpetuate his lineage. Childbearing was so important, that institutions such as polygamy (multiple wives), levirate marriage (when a brother married his deceased brother's widow if no sons were born prior to his death), and adoption were all established in order to save a father's life on earth.

But in spite of Leah's ability to produce, she still could not get Jacob's attention, affection, or affirmation. In spite of her ability to produce, Jacob still could not appreciate her strengths.

All of us have audiences that we just can't seem to please, who just can't seem to appreciate our strengths. For some of us it may be a parent for whom we could never do enough, for whom we could never seem to get it right. Our sibling was always the center of attraction. They were more intelligent, got better grades, had the lighter complexion, or were the life of the party.

For some of us it could be our spouse. We are faithful, we are diligent, we have forsaken all others and stuck by them through thick and thin—when they had work and couldn't work and wouldn't work, when they didn't have a car and now they have a car. We raised children, maintained a home, worked with a shoestring budget, and performed all of the duties as a spouse, but they just won't pay us any attention.

For some of us it is the ministry. We are articulate; we are strong, self-sufficient, creative, visionary, and gifted; and we add value wherever we are, but there are some audiences that will never appreciate our strengths because we are women.

For some of us, it is the job. We do all the work while somebody else makes all the money and gets all the credit. We do all the training while somebody else gets the promotion. There are some audiences that just can't appreciate our strengths.

For some of us our race keeps others from appreciating us. We are head and shoulders above our peers, we can run with the horses, we give 110%, we go the extra mile, we do what nobody else will, but our race keeps some audiences from appreciating our strengths.

And so Leah suffers from wounded self-esteem. Her self-esteem was wounded because she relied too much upon Jacob's estimation and evaluation of herself. Like Leah, so many of us suffer from wounded self-esteem because of someone else's evaluation of us.

Although self-esteem really refers to the estimation of our worth that we have of ourselves, many of us inherited the initial perception of ourselves from other sources—from the Jacobs and Labans in our lives—and we never bothered to consult God about our worth. So we suffer from impaired visions, holes in our soul, insecurity and mistaken identities. From the time of our birth, through early childhood, our adolescence, and even adulthood, other people impressed certain elements of identity upon us by the way they treated us and the way they talked to us.

Some of us have been coddled and cheered all of our lives and treated like royalty, while there are those of us who have been berated for our imperfections over which we had no control. Some of us know the experience of having strengths that were never appreciated because we were always being compared to someone else. We've been tolerated rather than celebrated.

We suffer from inferiority complexes, we feel that we are not good enough, and we fail to celebrate our value and our worth because of rejection from primary relationships. Consequently, many of us are not just emotionally fatigued but emotionally dependent. Emotional dependency is the condition where love and desperation for approval intersect—the belief that the ongoing presence and nurture of another person is necessary for security and self-worth.

And so, Leah illustrates the pain that we feel when "Jacob" won't notice us and it is revealed in the names that she gave her boys:

+ Reuben—"Because the Lord has *seen* my misery, and has given me a son as a sign of God's favor, maybe Jacob will love me now. I just want Jacob to see me, to just acknowledge my presence. I want to stop being treated as invisible."

+ Simeon—"Because the Lord *heard* that I am not loved, he gave me this one. I just want Jacob to hear me, to just give me an audience. He can hear everybody but me. Some of the advice that he esteems from others came from me first, but I can't get an audience with him."

+ Levi—"Because now maybe Jacob will become *attached* to me. Maybe there is hope for Jacob's affection. Now that I have given him three sons, maybe Jacob will become attached to me. Maybe Jacob will finally connect with me."

But in spite of three sons, in spite of her fertility, Jacob didn't see, Jacob didn't hear, and Jacob didn't attach himself to Leah.

What does one do with the emotional fallout that results from rejection by the primary audiences in our lives? What happens when the Jacob's in our lives don't change? The relevant question is, What do you do when folks don't change? What happens when reality does not line up with what we expected, what we hoped for, and even what we prayed for?

Most of us like stories that have happy endings, where the marriage is saved and we live happily ever after, where he falls hopelessly back in love with me and we live happily and securely without another outside interruption; where we are vindicated and the scales fall from folks' eyes and they finally see what they have been missing all these years; where folks can accept us for who we are and not penalize us because we are not Rachel. We like happy endings.

But we live in a real world where stories don't always have happy endings. We live in a real world where you do get breast cancer. We live in a real world where you can be faithful to a spouse and he or she will still have an affair. We live in a real world where you go to the doctor and the test still comes back positive. We live in a real world where some of our greatest dreams never materialize, a real world where folks will betray us and abandon us and disappoint us. We live in a real world where in spite of your best efforts folks reject us, a real world where you can invest everything you have in a relationship only to be left for someone who doesn't have half of your strengths. We live in a real world where stories don't always have happy endings, a real world where in spite of our strengths, in spite of all that we do, "Jacob" still doesn't change.

The question that I want to ask is, What do you do when Jacob doesn't change? Some things don't change. Some folks don't change. What do you when things and folks don't change? What do you do if Jacob don't change? And Jacob could be anyone whom we find ourselves emotionally dependent upon or attached to.

I see the answer in the text: one day, Leah experienced a defining moment that resulted in a change of attitude. Defining moments have the power to alter the entire trajectory of our lives. Defining moments are moments of truth in our lives that shift priorities and paradigms because we see reality from a different perspective. Defining moments are like intersections in our lives that give us options and opportunities to choose differently, think differently and act differently. Defining moments can put us on the path to becoming a new person.

Leah experienced a defining moment in her life that resulted in a change of attitude. The change of attitude changed her focus, changed her outlook, and reshaped her inner reality. There is a clue in the text that one day Leah must have come to the realization that she could no longer live her life dependent upon the ongoing nurture and approval of Jacob or wait on Jacob to change. One day Leah must have concluded that she could no longer jeopardize her emotional health by craving something she would probably never have.

By the time Leah gave birth to her fourth son, she was no longer consumed by her thoughts of Jacob. This time Leah had a reality check. Leah must have finally realized that she couldn't make Jacob love her, but she could love herself and most of all God loved her! Somewhere between verse 30 and verse 35, Leah gave birth to another son and a new Leah.

Verse 35 says that she conceived again, and when she gave birth to a son, she said, "This time I will praise the LORD." So she named him Judah. Then she stopped having children.

I believe Leah must have said to herself, "I had Reuben and Jacob didn't see me; I had Simeon and he didn't hear me; I even had Levi and he wouldn't become attached to me. But I can't worry about Jacob anymore. I cannot continue to live dependent upon the nurture and approval of Jacob. I can't live my life or see myself through Jacob's eyes. I can't be my best self-dependent upon the approval and acceptance of Jacob. I can't grow as long as I am obsessed with what someone else thinks about me. I cannot experience my potential as long as I keep investing my emotional and mental energy in a love-deficient relationship. I can't give myself away trying to measure up to somebody else's idea of what is acceptable. Jacob may not see me, he not hear me, and he won't even try to get know me, but thank God, God sees me, God hears me, and God has blessed me. And *this time I will praise the Lord*.

I believe that Leah decided, "Jacob may not love me. I may be tender-eyed. I may be the second choice. But if he never pays me a bit of attention, I am going to praise the Lord. I am not going to wait until Jacob accepts me. I am not waiting until somebody tells me I am good enough. I am not going to keep trying to earn somebody else's approval. I am not going to even worry about the fact that I am not Rachel. I am going to praise the Lord. Because being loved by God is greater than being loved by Jacob."

I believe that Leah decided: "My worth is not determined by Jacob. My value is not determined by my daddy or anybody else. My worth has is not based on what I look like or where I come from or what kind of clothes I wear. My worth doesn't even come from having somebody else's last name. My worth, my value comes from God."

And we too can say:

> I am fearfully and wonderfully made.
> I am God's masterpiece.
> I was created for good works.
> I am accepted by the Beloved.
> I am seated in heavenly places.
> I am the salt of the earth.
> I am the light of the world.
> I am a chosen generation.

I am a royal priesthood.

I am a new creation.

I am qualified to share in Christ's inheritance.

I am more than a conqueror.

I am a child of God.

I am chosen by God.

I am what God says I am.

I can be what God says I can be, I can do what God says I can, and I can have what God says I can have!

And even if Jacob don't change, I can change! I can live for the glory of God. I can recognize God's hand in my life. My life is bigger than my past, my mistakes, or my shortcomings. The God I serve will empower me to see not only who I am but what I am capable of becoming. The God I serve will empower me and strengthen me to live victoriously even if Jacob don't change!

CHAPTER 9

DO WHAT YOU CAN
WHILE YOU CAN

Now the Passover and the Festival of Unleavened Bread were only two days away, and the chief priests and the teachers of the law were scheming to arrest Jesus secretly and kill him. "But not during the festival," they said, "or the people may riot."

While he was in Bethany, reclining at the table in the home of Simon the Leper, a woman came with an alabaster jar of very expensive perfume, made of pure nard. She broke the jar and poured the perfume on his head.

Some of those present were saying indignantly to one another, "Why this waste of perfume? It could have been sold for more than a year's wages and the money given to the poor." And they rebuked her harshly.

"Leave her alone," said Jesus. "Why are you bothering her? She has done a beautiful thing to me. The poor you will always have with you, and you can help them any time you want. But you will not always have me. She did what she could. She poured perfume on my body beforehand to prepare for my burial. Truly I tell you, wherever the gospel is preached throughout the world, what she has done will also be told, in memory of her."

—MARK 14:1-9, NIV

IN HIS BOOK *LIVING A LIFE THAT MATTERS*, RABBI HAROLD Kushner states, "Most people are not afraid of dying, they are afraid of not having lived."[1] He writes: "It's not the prospect of death that frightens most people. People can accept the inescapable fact of mortality. What frightens them more is the dread of insignificance, the notion that we will be born and live and one day die and none of it will matter . . . that we will one day disappear, unheard of and unnoticed in an indifferent universe."[2]

Kushner further states: "The need to feel important drives people to place enormous value on such symbols as titles, corner offices, and first class travel. It causes us to feel excessively pleased when someone important recognizes us and to feel hurt when our doctor or pastor passes without saying hello, or when a neighbor calls us by our sister or brother names. The need to know that we are making a difference motivates doctors and medical researchers to spend hours looking through microscopes in the hope of finding cures for diseases. It drives inventors and entrepreneurs to stay up nights trying to find a better way of providing people with something they need. It causes artists, novelists and composers to try to add to the store of beauty in the world by finding just the right color, the right word, the right note. And it leads ordinary people to buy six copies of the local paper because it has their name or picture. It's what drives people to appear on daytime television shows revealing things about themselves and their families that most of us would be embarrassed to reveal to our pastor or closest friends. It may sound pitiful and others may scorn them, but for one hour they hold the attention of millions of viewers/ Americans."[3]

Because we find ourselves in so many settings that proclaim our insignificance—in stores where salespeople don't know our name, and don't care to know it; in crowded buses and airplanes that give us the message that if we weren't there someone else would be available to take our place—some people do desperate things to reassure themselves that they matter to the world. There are some who would argue that many innocent people across this nation and world have lost their lives sometimes in

part due to mental illness but also because of an insatiable desire on the part of the perpetrator to go to extreme measures to
see their names in print or in the headlines.

And while I do agree with Dr. Jerome Kagan, retired professor of psychology at Harvard, who said that the desire to
believe that the self is ethically worthy is universal, I have also
discovered that many of the persons who live lives that matter—those who inspire others to live, those who make the
world a better place, those who in the words of Ralph Waldo
Emerson leave the world a bit better, whether by a healthy
child, a garden patch, or a redeemed social condition—are not
always motivated by a desire for greatness or celebrity.

Dr. Cain Hope Felder once stated at a banquet honoring
persons for their pioneering work in the struggle for social justice and prophetic ministry: "One doesn't normally desire to be
a prophet. If you are ambitious enough, you will get a prophet's
reward and it won't be the kind of award that we are accus-
tomed to." Felder said that the prophet, "one who forth-tells
in God's name and functions as God's spokesperson commissioned to oppose oppression and collective unrighteousness or
the injustice of those in power and authority, is driven by the
Lord without regard for material consequences." He said it's a
life that is not your own, for a prophet stops living a life of one's
own.[4] And I would argue that people who live lives that matter
and impact the world do so by the small choices and decisions
they make a hundred times a day that add up to determine the
kind of world we live in and world that we impact.

Rosa Parks didn't necessarily set out to spark a movement,
although she had been attending the Highlander Training In-
stitute for Civil Rights; she was tired of giving in. Dr. Martin
Luther King Jr. didn't necessarily go to Montgomery to be the
president of the Montgomery Improvement Association and
assume the mantle of Civil Rights leader; he went to Montgomery, Alabama, to serve as the pastor of Dexter Avenue Baptist Church. Harriet Tubman didn't create the Underground

Railroad so that her name would be included in the annals of history as an abolitionist; she was a runaway slave who returned to the South 19 times to help lead over 300 slaves to freedom. Nelson Mandela didn't set out to become an apartheid activist, revolutionary, politician, and icon; he was simply directing a peaceful nonviolent campaign/protest against South African government and its racist policies.

And the woman in the text probably didn't break the jar of precious ointment on the head of Jesus because she expecting to be commended, criticized, immortalized, or prematurely eulogized; it was an act of extravagant worship, an expression of love and devotion toward Jesus whom she recognized as being more than just a carpenter.

The text says that she enters the home of Simon the Leper just two days before the Passover where Jesus was eating, while the Pharisees and religious leaders are plotting against him. Denied by one disciple, betrayed by another, and accused of rebellion and treason, with the cross looming before him, the woman performs one of the most important acts of honor that will take place. She crashes the party of all-male gathering, no doubt, and then takes a jar of precious ointment worth a year's wages and breaks the jar and pours the perfume on Jesus' head. Her gesture attracted the criticism of Jesus' male counterparts because they missed the symbolic significance of the woman's actions and interpreted her gesture as a waste. This unnamed, unapologetic, anonymous woman did not wait for someone to give her permission to do what she did. She acted courageously in obedience to God even at the risk of being misunderstood. There are many persons who have discovered that there are times when being misunderstood is the price we pay for our obedience to God. Perhaps it's a vision or a dream that God has given you. Perhaps it is being perceived as arrogant because of being confident about whom God made you to be. Maybe it is taking a radical step of obedience that seems strange to your family and peers? This is not to suggest that we should aspire to live our lives with the goal of being misunderstood, or that being misunderstood is always a sign that you are obeying God. But sometimes being misunderstood is the price we pay for our obedience to God. The woman in the text was misunderstood because of her obedience to God.

Although she seems to be no more than a footnote to the story because we have no biographical information, she creates a fundamentally different situation. This woman of no societal status stepped up with boldness and compassion and took a risk to worship Jesus in a manner fit for a king at a very pivotal moment in Jesus' life and ministry.

By this time, the Jewish authorities were secretly plotting to engineer the downfall of this radical offensive revolutionary who had consistently challenged the status quo, and his arrest was imminent. Very soon, Jesus would be tried on trumped -up charges and sentenced to a humiliating and excruciating crucifixion. But just before the catastrophe, this woman breaks the jar and anoints the head of Jesus.

And I believe she did it because despite the fact that she lived in a patriarchal society and was without status, significance, or access, she chose to honor Jesus *because she knew who she was ministering to*: she recognized Jesus as the Son of God. She saw clearly and knew supernaturally what to do because she knew who she was ministering to.

Notice that she doesn't anoint Jesus the way a person in those days would anoint a dead body. And indeed dead bodies were anointed as a sign of reverence and to assist in preservation in those days. Not only that, but a host would anoint his guests to refresh them, and sick people were anointed for healing. But when this woman anointed Jesus, Jesus wasn't dead, Jesus wasn't sick, and although it could have been for refreshment, the place that she anointed refutes this notion, because she didn't anoint Jesus' feet but she anointed his head. The woman performs the same ritual for Jesus that was performed by the prophet Samuel when he anointed Saul and David, for when they were anointed as kings, Samuel poured oil on their heads.

Dr. Cheryl Sanders says, "This woman demonstrated the courage of and the initiative of a prophet when she anointed Jesus' head with her precious ointment. She was willing to speak and act for God in symbolic action even when no one in the room understood her gesture of love."

We still live in a world that doesn't always understand gestures of love, particularly love for God. We live in a world where kindness is viewed with suspicion, mediocrity is celebrated, and excellence is despised.

The woman has seen something that others have not seen, and she knows something that others perhaps have preferred to deny: that Jesus is the Messiah, the anointed one, and, more, that he is destined to die. So despite being misunderstood, she broke the alabaster jar and anointed the head of Jesus with her perfume because she understood that while anointing served many purposes, in this case anointing the head belonged to the designation of kings. By her gesture, she recognizes that Jesus is not just Joseph's son, not just Mary's baby, not just the carpenter, not just the boy from the hood, but Jesus is the King of Israel. Her gesture of anointing Jesus on his head carries her clear understanding of his identity. She recognizes Jesus as Messiah.

The woman's insight, however, is both burden and grace. It is one thing to SEE, and it is another to do something with the knowledge one possesses. She SEES who Jesus is, and, more, she risks censure to demonstrate in a public way what she knows. The woman knew that she was not just anointing what would soon be a dead body or a corpse; she was anointing the head of a king. The Messianic secret of Mark had been revealed in an unexpected way to un-respected woman before it was revealed to the disciples.

And because of the revelation she received, she couldn't be guided by impulse or imitation, nor hindered by indecisiveness. Because she knew who Jesus was, she did not wait for anyone to give her permission to honor Jesus. She acted prophetically to minister to Jesus in a manner that was fit for a king even though her action would have been defined as inappropriate and out of order by her culture.

May I suggest that if you are going to do what you can and live a life that matters and do what you can while you can, not just to others, but to God, there will be times when ridicule and criticism may be the price that we pay for our obedience to God. It may be that we will be misunderstood, but go ahead and break the jar anyway.

King was criticized by many during his lifetime, but King didn't just give great speeches, King changed laws that changed the world. In fact, his book *Letter from the Birmingham Jail* is an open letter defending the strategy of nonviolent resistance to racism, arguing that people have a moral responsibility to break unjust laws. The Civil Rights Act of 1964 is the fruit of King's resolve, determination, persistence, and determination.

The discriminatory transit system of Montgomery, Alabama, was dismantled because of the collective protest of mostly black men and women in Montgomery, Alabama, who were mistreated and misunderstood. And while the world mourned the death of Nelson Mandela a few years ago, and celebrated him as an icon, hero, father, and ambassador for peace, the U.S. government officially considered him as a terrorist until 2008.

Gandhi was remembered in death as a grandfather-like pacifist, but in life he was viewed as an anti-colonial activist. Harriet Tubman was often under the sentence of death, and Rosa Parks went to jail, and they are only the ones that we know about. There are many others—an innumerable cloud of witnesses, reformers, and pioneers—who have made the world a better place because by their actions, like the woman with the alabaster jar, they were contrarian in their approach and they did what they could while they could.

So I need to say that there may be opposition. We may be criticized, and we may not get the support that we expect, but do it anyway. There will always be haters, detractors, critics, liars, and accusers, but make a decision to do live a life that matters to God and do what you can while you can.

And the rationale is in the text. Even though the woman had critics who felt that their argument was logical, Jesus told them they were wrong! Although they disapproved of her gesture and saw her gift as a waste, and her motives impure, Jesus helped them to see that while the opportunity to do ministry is always right and always available, the opportunity to minister to Jesus in a manner that is fit for a king would not be available again. And so rather than criticizing her actions, Jesus *defends* her actions.

Notice what Jesus said: "Leave her alone! Why are you bothering her? She has done a beautiful thing to me. The poor you will always have with you and you can help them anytime you want, but you will not always have me. She did what she could. It was intended that she use the perfume for this moment, and wherever the gospel is preached, what she has done will be told as a memorial to her."

The woman may have done many other good things in her life, but this moment happened to be the only reason she is known by virtually every believer. Because when she had the opportunity, she did what she could. She ministered to Jesus in a manner that was fit for a king because she recognized that Jesus was not just a carpenter but the Messiah who was the King of kings and Lord of lords.

And when you know who Jesus is, it's difficult not to do what you can. Despite the critics, despite the mediocrity of others, despite the indifference of others and the apathy of others, when you know who Jesus is, it's difficult not to do what you can.

So be like that woman: do what you can and go ahead and break your jar! Do what you can while you can! Jesus will defend your reputation and Heaven will back you up!

It's in the text. Just as Jesus told the woman's critics to leave her alone, Jesus will do the same thing for you. He'll condemn every tongue that rises up against you in judgment. He'll make your enemies your footstool. He'll prepare a table before you in the presence of your enemies. He'll defend your reputation.

So go ahead and honor Jesus and do what you can while you can. Because when you do, you walk in the tradition of Rosa and Nelson, Harriet and Martin, Esther and Rahab, Deborah and Miriam, Mary Magdalene and Joanna. But most of all, we walk in the tradition of Jesus, who did what he could while he could. His public ministry was only for three years, but in those three years he made an impact that is undeniable. He healed the sick, raised the dead, and gave sight to the blind. But most importantly he gave his life so that we might live.

Don't miss your chance to do something great for Jesus in your lifetime. Do what you can while you can. Windows of opportunity are limited. God has placed you where you are with the chance to use your resources and do something significant for him. Do what you can while you can because tomorrow is not promised. And we don't get a second chance to make a first impression. This ain't no dress rehearsal—this is it! So do what you can while you can!

NOTES

1. Harold S. Kushner, *Living a Life That Matters* (New York: Anchor Books, 2002), 146.

2. Ibid., 147.

3. Ibid., 7.

4. Cain Hope Felder, Honoree remarks at "Beautiful Are Their Feet" Banquet, Samuel Proctor Conference, February 20, 2013.

CHAPTER 10

WE'VE GOT NEXT

When the Sabbath was over, Mary Magdalene, Mary the mother of James, and Salome bought spices so that they might go to anoint Jesus' body. Very early on the first day of the week, just after sunrise, they were on their way to the tomb and they asked each other, "Who will roll the stone away from the entrance of the tomb?"

But when they looked up, they saw that the stone, which was very large, had been rolled away. As they entered the tomb, they saw a young man dressed in a white robe sitting on the right side, and they were alarmed.

"Don't be alarmed," he said. "You are looking for Jesus the Nazarene, who was crucified. He has risen! He is not here. See the place where they laid him. But go, tell his disciples and Peter, 'He is going ahead of you into Galilee. There you will see him, just as he told you.'"

Trembling and bewildered, the women went out and fled from the tomb. They said nothing to anyone, because they were afraid.

—MARK 16:1-8, NIV

THE WOMEN WHO WENT TO THE TOMB THAT FIRST EASTER morning were women whose lives had been touched by Christ. They had travelled with Jesus for three years, they heard him preach and teach, and they had witnessed his miracles and the signs he performed. They followed him to Calvary and then followed his body being carried by Joseph of Arimithea to the tomb in which he was laid.

These were brave women. They were women of courage. They knew they were risking their lives returning to the tomb in order to anoint the body of Jesus. And yet, they went to the tomb because all that they had lived for these the last three years had been taken away from them and they felt compelled to honor Jesus and give him a proper burial.

Bravely, Mary Magdalene, Mary the mother of James, and Salome came to the tomb that morning. Ironically, their biggest concern was not what they would find in the tomb or even the stench of a three-day dead body that would encounter. What worried them most was how they were going to roll the stone away. These were not timid and fearful women. Even after arriving at the tomb and seeing that the stone had been rolled away, both Marys and Salome walked in to the dark cavern, searching for the body of their Lord. But what they encountered there was more than they could have ever imagined! The tomb was empty! The place where they saw Joseph lay the body of Christ was empty!

And then all of a sudden there was a young man, dressed in a white robe, sitting where the body of Christ had been laid. "Don't be alarmed," he said, "You are looking for Jesus the Nazarene, who was crucified. He is risen! He is not here! See the place where they laid him." And then he continued to speak, "Go, tell his disciples and Peter, 'He is going ahead of you into Galilee. There you will see him, just as he told you.'"

But the women fled the tomb without saying a word! Throughout Mark's Gospel, Jesus had instructed people not to tell others about him. Now the women are told to tell the greatest message in the world and they say nothing!

Such an abrupt ending is rather perplexing for readers. In fact, the ending of Mark's Gospel has been a matter of considerable debate for some scholars. Many textual critics believe that the most reliable and earliest transcripts of the Gospel of

Mark end with verse 8 and that an editor later added two additional versions. Those who argue for a shorter ending base their conclusion primarily on internal evidence such as the differences in writing style and vocabulary. Newer translations of the Bible often have a note in the margin or a superscription, which says that the concluding verses of Mark are not found in the older manuscripts. Some manuscripts add a brief summary affirming that Jesus sent the disciples out on a mission to the world. The longer ending which is familiar to most people is comprised of verses 9-20 and combines elements of the resurrection appearance stories in the other Gospels or their traditions. There is an appearance to Mary Magdalene, an appearance to two disciples, and an appearance to the disciples during a meal in which Jesus castigates them for refusing to believe the witnesses to his resurrection and sends them on a worldwide mission and the ascension of Jesus. Elements of the apostolic tradition are also included in the longer ending: the ability to perform miracles, to speak in tongues, to handle deadly serpents, and to heal the sick, and Jesus' ascension into heaven after instructing his disciples.

Many scholars believe that the oldest manuscripts of Mark's Gospel do not end with all of the Resurrection hype and drama like the other Gospels. Instead, when Mary Magdalene and the other Mary meet the man at the tomb, he tells them that Jesus has been raised and sends them to remind the disciples of Jesus' earlier promise. But the shorter version of Mark says that the women flee and tell no one because they are afraid.

If this ending is indeed the most reliable and trustworthy ending, the obvious question becomes: Why would Mark end the story so abruptly? It seems peculiar that Mark would not include some account of Jesus' meeting with his disciples in Galilee or that he would not include some type of interaction with the women who came to anoint his dead body. To end the story at verse 8 is to leave "everything up in the air." It fails to bring closure to the story and provide it with something more uplifting and reassuring. The conclusion seems awkward and abrupt and creates both surprise and great suspense.

Furthermore, the response of the women seems so uncharacteristic. As devoted followers of Jesus, the last ones at the crucifixion and the first to come to the tomb, their response seems so uncharacteristic. It was the women who accompanied Jesus right from the start. They shared close personal contact with Jesus. They served Jesus as he served them. None of them were frightened at his arrest. All of them remained in close proximity to Jesus as he was condemned and executed. Even after Jesus' death, they were filled with Jesus' person and message.

One would have expected them to rush quickly from the tomb with great joy to report what they had heard to the disciples. But instead, in verse 8, Mark tells us that the women dash away in incoherent silence. There is no triumphalism, no trumpets blowing, no whistles sounding, and no confetti. Mark ends his account on a puzzling note: an empty tomb, a mysterious man declaring that Jesus has been raised but offering no proof, a promise of Jesus going ahead of his disciples to meet them in Galilee, and the women too scared to say or do anything.

This strange and dissatisfying ending does not seem to be an appropriate way to end a story that is supposed to be about good news. It also does not seem to be an appropriate response from women who enjoyed a unique relationship of liberating acceptance with Jesus.

Instead of triumph, we encounter terror and confusion. We expect that something good is going to happen when the women find that the stone has been rolled away from the tomb, but it does not. The young man does not announce, "Surprise, Hallelujah He is not here." Instead he greets them with the words: "Don't be alarmed. You are looking for Jesus the Nazarene who was crucified. He has risen! He is not here. See the place where they laid him. But go, tell his disciples and Peter, 'He is going ahead of you into Galilee. There you will find him, just as he told you.' Trembling and bewildered, the women went out and fled the tomb. They said nothing to anyone, because they were afraid."

Why does Mark end this story with women too frightened to speak? Why are the women afraid now? Why would they be so reluctant to keep the greatest news of all a secret?

All through Mark's Gospel the Messianic secret (a code of silence) has been a prevalent issue. In Mark's Gospel, Jesus stressed the importance of not telling anyone what he did. When Jesus healed the deaf and mute man he commanded them not to tell anyone (Mark 7:36). When Jesus healed those with unclean spirits, he charged them that they should tell no one (Mark 3:12). When Jesus raised the ruler of the synagogue's daughter from the dead, he charged them no man should know what he had done (Mark 5:43). When Peter declared that Jesus was the Christ, Jesus charged the disciples not to tell anyone about him (Mark 8:30).

Throughout Mark's Gospel, emphasis is placed upon this code of silence by those who witnessed Jesus miracles. Now when Jesus' followers are finally told to speak about Jesus, they say nothing to anyone. Why are the women so afraid? Furthermore, why does their fear lead to silence? The text says that the women fled the tomb and said nothing to anyone because they were afraid. Why is there silence now that they finally have the opportunity to speak up? Furthermore, why is there silence from Jesus' most loyal supporters?

It is helpful to understand what it meant for the women to carry a message of good news about a Palestinian Jew who challenged the status quo. During Jesus' life and even in death, good news could cause unnecessary trouble. In fact, it was good news that always seems to create trouble for Jesus. Good news created trouble for Jesus:

+ When he preached his trial sermon in the synagogue from Isaiah (Luke 4:28-30)

+ When he forgave the sin of a woman caught in the very
  act of adultery (John 8:58)
+ When he dared to cure a man with a withered hand on
  the Sabbath (Mark 3:6)
+ When he commanded the unclean spirits out of a man
  and into a herd of swine (Mark 5:17)

In those days good news could get you in trouble. And when Mark wrote this Gospel, he was writing to people who were living under stressful times. People were facing major crises. Christians had to cope with the death of eyewitnesses.

Being a Christian meant being subjected to vicious gossip and hostility. It meant deflecting government suspicion because they were always viewed as a potentially subversive group. They had to defend themselves against church rivals who would foil the church's growth. Christians were misrepresented as atheists and haters of humankind. They were framed by false witnesses and trumped-up charges and betrayed by their friends. The audience that Mark wrote to was an audience that faced persecution, suffering, and death.

So the resurrection did not mean that everything had been set right and that everybody would live "happily ever after." Jesus had already made it clear that after the resurrection, his followers would be living in a period of woes. There would be wars, persecution, betrayal, tribulation, and deception. If they proclaimed the good news, Jesus promised that they would be hated by all. Perhaps the women were afraid to say anything to anyone because the resurrection didn't just mean victory over death but it also meant persecution. Therefore fear could be an appropriate response for the women, not because they failed but because they were human. Perhaps that is why the women left the tomb in silence, because they knew that as good as the news was it could mean persecution or even cost them their lives.

Mark gives us a glimpse of their apprehension when he says that, trembling and bewildered, the women went out and fled from the tomb. They said nothing to anyone because they were afraid.

But perhaps we shouldn't be too hard on these women. Truth be told, we too know the consequences of taking up the cross of Jesus, for anyone who really decides to journey with Jesus knows the danger of crossing to the other side. As Eugene Peterson states in his book, *A Long Obedience in the Same Direction*, "THIS WORLD IS NO FRIEND TO GRACE. A person who makes a commitment to Jesus Christ as Lord and Savior does not find a crowd immediately forming to applaud the decision or old friends spontaneously gathering around to offer congratulations and counsel. Ordinarily there is nothing directly hostile, but an accumulation of puzzled disapproval and agnostic indifference constitutes, nevertheless, surprisingly formidable opposition."[1]

Perhaps this is why there have been attempts to append the happier endings. The shorter version of Mark does not leave us with a neat resolution, but with a terrifying ultimatum: meet him in Galilee, the place where the disciples were first called to follow. Perhaps Mark did leave us hanging for a reason. Perhaps he intended for us to finish the story.

We don't really need Mark to tell us what else happened. We already know that something happened. We have the book of Acts, Paul's letters, Peter's letters, Hebrews, and Revelation to tell us what happened next. The Resurrection is not the end of the story, but the beginning, for the resurrection sets in motion a new story that is not yet finished or resolved. It will not be completed until the elect are gathered from the ends of the earth. What happens next is really up to us as believers. Mark didn't tell us what happened next. He told us what we had to *do* next. The text says in verse 7: "But go your way, tell his disciples and Peter that he goeth before you into Galilee: there shall you see him, as he said unto you."

When God raised Jesus from the dead, and transformed his body, God ushered in a new order of existence. What belongs to the future kingdom of God, the glorious age to come, has made its appearance in this present evil age. How will we respond now that we have been let in on the news? We know enough to make a proclamation: The tomb is empty, Hallelujah, and Christ is risen! How will we respond now that we know that the tomb is empty? Will we tell anybody the good news? Or will we flee in fear and become silent? Now that we know the story, we cannot afford to keep silent. In a world of moral collapse, moral values gone amuck, violence, killing, and religious and racial intolerance, will the story die with us, or will we obediently follow Jesus into Galilee?

My suspicion is that the women had to have said something to someone. Although they were initially afraid, their fear did not last. Fear may have initially driven them from the tomb in terror, but they had to have spoken because they were the first witnesses to the resurrection. How else would the disciples know to go to Galilee? Perhaps the women never got over their fear but they eventually moved forward in spite of their fear. And this is the challenge that gospel presents to us.

As fearful as we might be of proclaiming the gospel, it is a gospel worth proclaiming. The tomb is empty! Hallelujah and Christ is risen! It is this gospel that is more powerful than our fears. For the God who raised Jesus from the dead can raise us out of fear so that we too can respond to the words of God's messenger despite our fears and proclaim to the world: Jesus is risen! Go and meet him in Galilee! We've got next!

NOTE

1. Eugene H. Peterson, *A Long Obedience in the Same Direction: Discipleship in an Instant Society* (Downers Grove, IL: IVP Books, 2000).

OTHER PUBLICATIONS
by MMGI BOOKS

* * *

THESE SISTERS CAN SAY IT! VOLUME 1
Edited by Cynthia L. Hale and Darryl D. Sims

THESE SISTERS CAN SAY IT! VOLUME 2
Edited by Martha Simmons and Darryl D. Sims

THE GOSPEL ACCORDING TO CANCER
By Patricia Gould Champ

STRONGER IN MY BROKEN PLACES
By Charles E. Booth

NAVIGATING PASTORAL LEADERSHIP IN THE TRANSITION ZONE
By D. Darrell Griffin

STANDING ON HOLY COMMON GROUND: AN AFRICENTRIC
MINISTRY APPROACH TO PROPHETIC COMMUNITY ENGAGEMENT
By Lester A. McCorn

ADAM COME HOME: LIBERATING THE MINDS OF BLACK MEN
By Darryl D. Sims

EVANGELIZING AND EMPOWERING THE BLACK MALE
Edited by Darryl D. Sims

* * *

Order your copies today!
Online at mmgibooks.com and at Amazon.com

For discounts on bulk orders, please call
773.314.7060